Tim Witmer's *The Shepherd* [...]
Now comes the sequel, *The S[...] Toolbox*, which is so good
for helping me to get my hands around the practical aspects of
church leadership—everything from church planting to using
technology to enduring in the hard times. Very helpful for the
plumbing, plowing, and carpentry of everyday ministry.
—**Bryan Chapell**, Stated Clerk, Presbyterian Church in America

If you were helped by reading *The Shepherd Leader* by Timothy
Witmer, then you are going to love this companion to his important work. *The Shepherd's Toolbox* is the ideal follow-up to Witmer's
classic work for two reasons. First, it takes his biblical principles
of shepherding and makes them practical. Second, it gathers
proven pastoral voices from a variety of churches to prove that
his shepherding convictions are applicable in any church context.
Every pastor who desires to understand how to shepherd in his
specific church scenario and how to do so practically needs to
read this book and read it with his fellow elders.
—**Brian Croft**, Executive Director, Practical Shepherding

Tim Witmer has long served the church by helping pastors to
understand and live out their God-given roles. In this valuable
book, Witmer orchestrates a team of leaders who answer pressing
questions on topics such as how to best set up effective shepherding structures and wise ways to care for women.
—**Daniel M. Doriani**, Professor of Biblical Theology, Covenant Theological Seminary; Founder and Director, Center of
Faith and Work, St. Louis

As a longtime pastor, I recognize how challenging are the demands
placed upon the elders of a local congregation. The priority of
"shepherd[ing] the flock of God that is among you" (1 Peter 5:2)

can quickly shift to the background amid myriad other pressing needs and concerns. *The Shepherd's Toolbox* shows us that there is a path forward for leaders, both men and women, whose hearts are guided by the Chief Shepherd and who are eager to care for their flocks. This book is eminently practical for churches that want to learn how to implement a congregation-wide shepherding strategy. I cannot recommend this highly enough!

—**Thomas C. Gibbs**, President, Covenant Theological Seminary

The One who is gentle and lowly in heart, our Good Shepherd, wants to be experienced as such through the people who provide hands-on care for his sheep. The authors of this book do an excellent job of helping us to form ministries that make this not only possible but likely.

—**Scott Sauls**, Senior Pastor, Christ Presbyterian Church, Nashville; Author, *A Gentle Answer* and *Beautiful People Don't Just Happen*

The Shepherd's Toolbox is a wonderful supplement to Tim Witmer's *The Shepherd Leader*, which has been used by a number of church leaders to start or reimagine shepherding programs within their churches. Our church has benefited greatly from the ministry of our men and women shepherds. I personally don't know how a large church like ours would have weathered the COVID pandemic if our shepherds hadn't cared for and connected with our flock. This supplement is a great addition to Witmer's original work as it gives churches real-life examples of shepherding ministry challenges and successes and creates a more detailed road map for them.

—**Clay Smith**, Senior Pastor, Central Presbyterian Church, St. Louis

THE
SHEPHERD'S
TOOLBOX

THE SHEPHERD'S TOOLBOX

Advancing Your Church's
Shepherding Ministry

EDITED BY
TIMOTHY Z. WITMER

PUBLISHING
P.O. BOX 817 • PHILLIPSBURG • NEW JERSEY 08865-0817

Unless otherwise indicated, Scripture quotations are from the ESV® Bible (The Holy Bible, English Standard Version®), copyright © 2001 by Crossway, a publishing ministry of Good News Publishers. Used by permission. All rights reserved.

The Scripture quotation marked (BSB) is from The Holy Bible, Berean Standard Bible, BSB. Copyright © 2016, 2020 by Bible Hub. Used by Permission. All Rights Reserved Worldwide.

The Scripture quotation marked (CSB) is from The Christian Standard Bible. Copyright © 2017 by Holman Bible Publishers. Used by permission. Christian Standard Bible®, and CSB® are federally registered trademarks of Holman Bible Publishers, all rights reserved.

Scripture quotations marked (NIV) are from the Holy Bible, New International Version®, NIV®. Copyright © 1973, 1978, 1984, 2011 by Biblica, Inc.™ Used by permission of Zondervan. All rights reserved worldwide. www.zondervan.com. The "NIV" and "New International Version" are trademarks registered in the United States Patent and Trademark Office by Biblica, Inc.™

Italics within Scripture quotations indicate emphasis added.

ISBN: 978-1-62995-531-5 (pbk)
ISBN: 978-1-62995-534-6 (ePub)

Printed in the United States of America

Library of Congress Cataloging-in-Publication Data has been applied for.

To church leaders around the world
whose love for the Chief Shepherd is
seen in their care for the sheep
entrusted to them

CONTENTS

LIST OF USER GUIDES

PREFACE

WHEN THE TENTH anniversary of *The Shepherd Leader* was drawing near, my publisher and I discussed releasing an updated edition of the book. In God's providence, since its publication hundreds of churches have used the book to create new shepherding plans or improve existing ones. *The Shepherd Leader* has also reached an international audience, having been translated into Chinese, Korean, Russian, and Spanish, with other translations in process.

Why has this book been gobbled up by so many? The answer is that those who are called to be leaders in the church *know* that they are to be shepherds of their flocks, and many (most?) of their efforts have been mired in the slough of despond. In the past, many leaders initiated shepherding strategies for their flocks and then gave up for one reason or another. *The Shepherd Leader* provided not only the biblical imperative for this work but a practical plan to get started.

So why *The Shepherd's Toolbox* and not a new edition of *The Shepherd Leader*? We decided *The Shepherd's Toolbox* would be a more useful supplement to the original volume. Why? Since the release of *The Shepherd Leader,* faithful leaders have put its principles into practice and, more importantly, have addressed some of the challenges of establishing a shepherding strategy. This volume contains some of the best practices that have arisen in overcoming some of the thornier obstacles facing those who are committed to shepherding their flocks.

Here is an overview of what follows.

The first chapter addresses the proper motivation for shepherding the flock. Don't skip this chapter, as it lays the groundwork for the rest of the book. Part 1, Shaping a Shepherding Structure, begins with a chapter from Ken Jones, previously shepherding pastor at Oak Mountain Presbyterian Church (Birmingham, Alabama), who describes structures that support a team-based approach to caring for members. In chapter 3, ruling elder Gary L. Smith (St. Louis, Missouri) describes the process of helping ruling elders to become invested in a shepherding ministry. In chapter 4, executive pastor John Barrett (Augusta, Georgia) provides encouragement to persevere as he gives an honest assessment of how his church started and restarted its shepherding ministry over the years.

Part 2 focuses on one of the greatest challenges that faces every congregation: Shepherding Every Member. In chapter 5, pastor of shepherding Randy Schlichting (Atlanta, Georgia) explains how technology assisted the elders of his church in caring for all 4,500 of their members. This should be of particular interest to larger churches, though there is application for churches of any size. Chapter 6, written by Bijan Mirtolooi (London, England), former pastor in charge of community groups and pastoral care at Redeemer Presbyterian West Side in New York City, delves into the use of small groups in shepherding. In chapter 7, women's ministry director Sue Harris (Birmingham, Alabama), addresses a common oversight in our ministries as she shares a strategy for caring for the women of the church.

Part 3 considers an often-neglected implication of our work: Shepherding and Advancing the Gospel. In chapter 8, lead pastor Mark Hallock (Englewood, Colorado) describes the importance of implementing shepherding care to advance church planting.

In chapter 9, I offer a concluding challenge to remember to reach out to the lost sheep who have yet to respond to the voice of the Good Shepherd.

As I recounted in my previous book, while researching *The Shepherd Leader* I visited Bob and Betty Herr, friends of mine who kept a large flock of sheep in Lancaster County, Pennsylvania. They helped me to understand a lot about sheep, and I had been able to integrate what I learned into the book. When it was published, I personally delivered a few copies to them so that they could see the fruit of our labors.

As I entered the lane and looked into the pasture, I saw no sheep. Maybe they were all in the barn for some reason? When Bob and Betty came to greet me, I asked where the sheep had gone.

"We sold all the sheep," Bob said.

I was startled. "Why would you do that?" I asked.

"We only have goats," Bob replied. "The sheep were too hard to take care of."

Sure enough, as I left, I saw that the sign at the end of the lane had been changed. It used to say, "Nix Besser Sheep," with a cute little sheep face painted in the middle. Now the sign says, "Nix Besser Goats," with a cute little goat face.

Shepherding the flock can be challenging. But this is our calling. These are the ones for whom the Good Shepherd gave his life. These are the ones for whom we are called to care. And, sobering but true, these are the ones for whom we will have to give an account one day. The contributors and I pray that this book will encourage you as you care for the sheep entrusted to you. But remember that no one is more enthusiastic about your labors as a shepherd than the Chief Shepherd himself. This is why he promises that when he appears, "you will receive the unfading crown of glory" (1 Peter 5:4).

READ THIS FIRST:
MOTIVATION FOR SHEPHERDS

TIMOTHY Z. WITMER

HAVE YOU EVER been confronted by the challenge of assembling something complicated? Even before you gather the tools for the job, it helps to turn to the material labeled "Read This First." Here we typically find helpful hints and directions for how to proceed. I've learned my lesson the hard way several times after failing to consult these instructions. *Stumbling* and *bumbling* are the right words to characterize my efforts, not to mention *hand-wringing frustration*!

When you picked up this book, perhaps the first thing you did was scan the table of contents to see what might be most interesting or helpful to you. There is indeed a lot of helpful material in the pages to come. But as we begin, we must address the *motivation* behind everything that follows. When Jesus met the frustrated fishermen on the Sea of Galilee a short time after his resurrection, he knew how important it was to reset their motivation for ministry.

Do You Love the Good Shepherd?

It was after a long night of fruitless fishing that Peter came face-to-face with the risen Christ. The Chief Shepherd had come to restore his wandering sheep to the fold and to renew his call on Peter and deploy him once more for kingdom purposes. In obedience to the shadowy figure on the shoreline, Peter and the other disciples cast their nets into the water and suddenly brought in a haul of flopping fish.

After breakfast, the important conversation began.

"Do you love me?" Jesus asked. If it had been me, I would have asked, "Peter, what were you thinking?" or "Peter, how could you mess up so badly?" But Jesus knew exactly what he was doing. Three times he asked his dense disciple if he loved him. Although Peter became upset by the repetition, he nonetheless affirmed his love for his Savior each time. Only after each affirmation of love did Jesus charge him, "Feed my lambs. . . . Tend my sheep. . . . Feed my sheep" (John 21:15–17). Not only does this exchange remind us that ministry is about the sheep, but it reminds us that love for Christ is the essential motivation for ministry.

Archibald Alexander writes that a shepherd of the flock is "nothing—or at best a mere 'sounding brass or tinkling cymbals'" if he lacks "supreme love of Christ. . . . Genius, learning, eloquence, zeal, public exertion, and great sacrifices—even if it should be all of our goods and of our lives themselves—will be accounted of no value in the eyes of the Lord if love to Christ be wanting."[1] Each of us must admit that our ministry may often be motivated by something other than love for Christ. In particular, it may

1. Archibald Alexander, "The Pastoral Office," in *Princeton and the Work of the Christian Ministry*, ed. James M. Garretson (Edinburgh: Banner of Truth Trust, 2012), 1:256. Punctuation has been modernized.

flow from a desire to meet the usual metrics of success—such as a balanced budget and growing attendance—and to receive the accompanying accolades. Peter himself warned against these motivators when he wrote to his fellow elders,

> Shepherd the flock of God that is among you, exercising oversight, not under compulsion, but willingly, as God would have you; not for shameful gain, but eagerly; not domineering over those in your charge, but being examples to the flock. (1 Peter 5:2–3)

Perhaps your motivation for ministry has faded and shepherding seems like just something else to do, yet another burden on top of everything else. If that's the case, let me encourage you to take steps to renew your first love.

Remember His Call to Faith

Jesus undoubtedly designed elements of the incident by the Sea of Galilee to remind Peter of their first meeting in Luke 5:1–11. What was Peter doing at that time? He was fishing. How many fish had he caught? None. What did Jesus instruct him to do? Put the nets down again. What happened? The nets were filled with flopping fish. The John 21 encounter would have reminded Peter of the moment when he first fell down on his knees at Jesus's feet—a moment of understanding and faith that changed his life forever. But after the seaside breakfast, Jesus repeatedly addressed Peter as "Simon, son of Jonah." This was the name his parents had given to him—not "Simon Peter," the name Jesus had given to him.

For us to renew our love for Christ, we must remember who we were and what we were before he called us to himself. I was a self-confident performance major in a school of music that required us to be *very* sure of ourselves, to say the least. Then the knock came on my door, both literally and figuratively. The literal knock was from an upperclassman music major who came to talk to me about Jesus. He was a member of a Christian ministry on campus and rightly suspected that I needed something more than my musical talent to be satisfied in this life and ready for the life to come.

My parents had faithfully taken me to church as a child, and as the student shared the good news with me, I knew I had heard these things before. But then he asked if I had ever personally believed, if I had ever received the amazing gifts of forgiveness and everlasting life for myself. This was not merely good news—it was really new to me! When I responded to the Spirit's knock on the door of my heart that day, little did I know that an amazing journey had begun. Part of the journey has been growth in understanding the extent of God's grace in giving his Son for me, a pursuit that will continue throughout eternity.

To renew our love in any relationship, it is often beneficial for us to remember how it all began: the circumstances, places, and conversations that surrounded it. It's the reason I take my wife each year to the place where we went on our first date. Our relationship with the Lord is no different; we renew our love for him when we remember that we love him because he first loved us. David Powlison puts it well: "[God's love] is at God's initiative and choice; it isn't given out on the basis of my performance. God's gospel love is not wages that I earn with a model life; it is a gift. It is a gift that I cannot earn; more than that, it is a gift that I do not even deserve. God loves weak, ungodly, sinful enemies. The gift is the opposite of what I deserve. God ought to kill me on the spot. Instead, He sent His Son to die in my place."[2] These are simple yet profound truths to which we need to return.

When was the last time you meditated on the grace God demonstrated in the circumstances that he used to draw you to himself? When was the last time you thanked him for the people who were faithful to share the good news with you? Take a moment to do those things!

Another important influence in my college days was a retired missionary who served as a "dorm mom" in my wife-to-be's dorm. Hazel took my future wife and me under her wing and invited us to her apartment for home-cooked meals. After every meal, she opened her Bible and began to teach us. She didn't ask permission, but her instruction was as natural and satisfying as dessert. Hazel used to describe a person's testimony as their "story," and if she met another Christian, she would ask them about it.

When is the last time you shared your story with your church or with your family? Have you shared it with your children? If you are blessed to have grandchildren, have they heard your testimony? The apostle Paul recounts his story three times in the book of Acts and alludes to it several times throughout his letters. He writes to the Corinthians that "by the grace of God I am what I am" (1 Cor. 15:10). So it was for Paul and for Peter. So it is for you.

Just as the circumstances of John 21 reminded Peter of the day the Savior initially called him to faith, may you be reminded of the time when you first heard the Good Shepherd's voice, began to follow him, and were assured of forgiveness and eternal life. This will fan the flame of your love for Christ and better motivate you to shepherd the flock. May his question and his command resonate in your heart: Do you love me? Feed my lambs.

---

2. David Powlison, *Seeing with New Eyes: Counseling and the Human Condition through the Lens of Scripture* (Phillipsburg, NJ: P&R Publishing, 2003), 167.

Remember His Call to Serve

Peter's call to faith and his call to serve as an apostle were virtually simultaneous. When he responded to Jesus in faith in Luke 5, Jesus called him to be a fisher of men in the same encounter. When Jesus renewed his call to Peter in John 21, he expanded that call from fishing for men to caring for the flock.

When we as elders consider what motivates us to shepherd the flock, we must remember that it is Christ who has called us to serve in this office. When Paul reunited with his beloved elders in Miletus, he reminded them, "Pay careful attention to yourselves and to all the flock, *in which the Holy Spirit has made you overseers*, to care for the church of God, which he obtained with his own blood" (Acts 20:28). The remarkable privilege and responsibility of caring for the flock was not something the elders took on themselves because they thought it was a good idea. No, the Holy Spirit made them overseers. It was the call of the Good Shepherd through the Spirit that brought them to this place of service. In the same way, you have not become a leader in the church because *you* thought it was a good idea. Remember that it was the risen Lord who called you.

Unlike Peter, who was called simultaneously to faith and to service, most of us experience gradual and progressive growth in our grasp of the call to office in the church. In my case, a few years passed between the knock that led to my conversion and my realization that God was calling me to be a shepherd of his flock.

Many factors led me to recognize God's call. First, the Lord opened the doors of ministry experience. I started by serving in the campus ministry through which I had heard the good news. Then came the opportunity for me to take on the role of youth leader in a local church. There I discovered I had some gifting in the areas of public ministry. This was confirmed by the people whom I served.

Theologians refer to the dynamic I've described as the *external call*—that is, the confirmation by others that the Lord may be leading a person to church office. The consummation of the external call comes when a man's gifts and calling are confirmed through ordination by an ecclesial body. If you are a pastor, this confirmation comes through a presbytery or another church authority. If you are a ruling elder, this comes via a local congregation.

The external call is an important part of the journey toward ordination. Of equal importance, however, is what is referred to as the *internal call*. This is the inclination of the heart to serve in a church office. This is why Paul refers to those who "[*aspire*] to the office" of elder (1 Tim. 3:1). You can have all the affirmation in the world from others, but if the Spirit has not put an internal burden on you to serve, it would be a huge mistake for you to move forward. Martyn Lloyd-Jones wrote that "this is something that happens to you; it is God dealing with you, and God acting upon you by His Spirit; it is something you become aware of rather than what you do. It is thrust upon you, it is presented to you and almost forced upon you constantly in this way."[3] For me, this conviction grew over time to the point that I became convinced that the Lord was calling me to aspire to the pastoral office.

Take a few minutes to reflect on the circumstances and people who influenced you to aspire to serve as an officer in the church. Be sure to think about the Spirit's work on your heart as well. Perhaps you were reluctant at first but over time became

3. D. Martyn Lloyd-Jones, *Preachers and Preaching* (Grand Rapids: Zondervan, 1971), 104.

convinced that God's call to you included a call to become a shepherd of his flock.

If you find that your motivation is lacking, take some time—perhaps a whole day—to reflect on the Lord's call to faith and his call to serve. As it came to Peter that chilly morning in Galilee, the question comes to *you* again: Do you love me? Tend my sheep.

Remember His Grace to You

As we have seen, when the Good Shepherd came to restore his wandering sheep in John 21, he chose a context that would remind Peter of his conversion and call. But he also chose a setting that would remind Peter of his boastful failures. When Peter denied his Lord three times in succession, he was warming himself by a fire in the courtyard. Here was another fire. He denied his Lord in the cool of the evening; Jesus came to speak to him in the cool of the morning. But then Jesus gave him three opportunities to affirm his love for the Savior whom he had denied three times on that darkest of dark nights.

In the upper room on the night of his arrest, Jesus had warned his disciples, "You will all fall away because of me this night. For it is written, 'I will strike the shepherd, and the sheep of the flock will be scattered'" (Matt. 26:31). In response, Peter boldly proclaimed, "Though they all fall away because of you, I will never fall away" (v. 33). Jesus immediately confronted him with these haunting words: "Truly, I tell you, this very night, before the rooster crows, you will deny me three times" (v. 34). But Peter doubled down and said, "Even if I must die with you, I will not deny you!" (v. 35).

Of course, Peter did not live up to his boast. But Jesus didn't return to Galilee to say, "I told you so." Rather he reminded Peter of his words in John 10:

> My sheep hear my voice, and I know them, and they follow me.
> I give them eternal life, and they will never perish, and no one
> will snatch them out of my hand. My Father, who has given
> them to me, is greater than all, and no one is able to snatch
> them out of the Father's hand. (vv. 27–29)

As one of Jesus's sheep, Peter would never be lost, but he needed
Jesus to seek him out and restore him so that he could be in a
right relationship with his Master.

Peter was learning that there was only one Messiah—and it
wasn't him! Paul Tripp wrote, "You are called to be a public and
influential ambassador of a glorious King, but you must resist
the desire to be a king. You are called to trumpet God's glory,
but you must never take that glory for yourself. You are called to
a position of leadership, influence, and prominence, but in that
position you are called to 'humble yourself under the mighty
hand of God.'"[4] Tripp is referring to Peter's first letter, where
Peter continues,

> Humble yourselves, therefore, under the mighty hand of God
> so that at the proper time he may exalt you, casting all your
> anxieties on him, because he cares for you. (1 Peter 5:6–7)

Peter was learning about the kingdom value of downward mobil-
ity. He was learning the way of the cross.

As you consider what motivates you to shepherd the flock,
ask yourself if your zeal has waned because you have wandered.
Remember, though, that Jesus loves you and forgives you when
you come to him with a repentant heart. You will recall that when

---

4. Paul David Tripp, *Dangerous Calling: Confronting the Unique Challenges of
Pastoral Ministry* (Wheaton: Crossway Books, 2012), 214.

Peter generously offered to forgive "seven times," Jesus dramatically inflated that number to "seventy-seven times" (Matt. 18:21, 22). Remember to preach to yourself what you have preached and taught to others. Do not doubt God's mercy! Do not doubt his grace! Do not doubt his Word! Edward Welch asks us, "Do you ever think, 'How could God forgive me for *that!*' (whatever *that* is)? Do you think that God's forgiveness is a begrudging forgiveness? Do you think that God's promises are only for other people, who haven't done what you have done? . . . The truth is that your own sins, no matter how big, are not beyond the blood of Jesus or bigger than God's pleasure in forgiveness."[5]

Don't allow yourself to be spiritually "dead in the water" over the sin that remains in your life. Satan would be very happy to see you immobilized and useless. Peter spoke from experience when he wrote, "Be sober-minded; be watchful. Your adversary the devil prowls around like a roaring lion, seeking someone to devour" (1 Peter 5:8). On another occasion, Jesus had told him,

> Simon, Simon, behold, Satan demanded to have you, that he might sift you like wheat, but I have prayed for you that your faith may not fail. And when you have turned again, strengthen your brothers. (Luke 22:31–32)

Peter fell, but his faith did not fail. Would he fail again? Yes. Will you fail again? Yes, but your Lord is faithful. Jesus walked to Galilee to restore Peter. He comes to *you* to invite your repentance and to welcome you back; he is determined to restore and forgive you.

5. Edward T. Welch, *When People Are Big and God Is Small: Overcoming Peer Pressure, Codependency, and the Fear of Man*, 2nd ed. (Phillipsburg: NJ: P&R Publishing, 2023), 149–50.

If you are struggling, you are not alone. You can be assured that Jesus is praying for you too—this time from his exalted place at the right hand of the Father. The Lord is with you, and there are many to whom you can reach out for counsel and prayer. The loving Chief Shepherd seeks his lost sheep. Perhaps he is seeking you right now.

As we reflect on God's grace in calling us and restoring us, our love for him grows, and so should our motivation to shepherd the flock. "Do you love me? Feed my sheep."

Do You Love His Sheep?

In John 21, Jesus does not explicitly mention loving the sheep as a motivating factor for caring for them. However, love for others is a fundamental mark of the Christian.

> A new commandment I give to you, that you love one another: just as I have loved you, you also are to love one another. By this all people will know that you are my disciples, if you have love for one another. (John 13:34–35).

Not only that, but Jesus made it clear that the leaders in his kingdom are to be marked by service as well as love:

> You know that the rulers of the Gentiles lord it over them, and their great ones exercise authority over them. It shall not be so among you. But whoever would be great among you must be your servant, and whoever would be first among you must be your slave, even as the Son of Man came not to be served but to serve, and to give his life as a ransom for many. (Matt. 20:25–28)

Shortly after my retirement from forty-two years of full-time pastoral ministry, someone asked me, "What was the most wonderful part about pastoral ministry?" I replied, "The people." Then I was asked, "What was the most challenging part of pastoral ministry?" My reply? "The people." As leaders, we are called to serve the sheep despite the trouble they may cause. There must never be any doubt that we are there to serve the sheep and not vice versa. After all, these precious ones are those whom "he obtained with his own blood" (Acts 20:28). They are not our sheep; they are his sheep. He calls us to serve them and to love them. There is no doubt that some sheep make this commandment very difficult to follow. This is when you need to remember God's patience with *you*, one of his sheep, and his gracious forgiveness toward *you*, a member of his flock.

Conclusion

Peter would not receive thrones or accolades in this life. Immediately after charging him to shepherd the flock, Jesus said, "'Truly, truly, I say to you, when you were young, you used to dress yourself and walk wherever you wanted, but when you are old, you will stretch out your hands, and another will dress you and carry you where you do not want to go.' (This he said to show by what kind of death he was to glorify God)" (John 21:18–19).

You may not be called to be a martyr, but as a leader you are called to give your life for the flock in other ways: to sacrifice your time to care for their needs, to share their emotional burdens as you walk with them through the valley of the shadow of death, to bear the anxiety that fills your heart when you must admonish a sheep who is straying. The strength to persevere in your calling is found in the renewal of your first love for Christ.

Shepherding is challenging and rewarding—but it won't bring you the rewards that are often coveted in this world. This is why proper motivation for ministry is so important. Its reward in this life is the joy of serving the One who died for you when you serve those he has entrusted to your care. Jesus's final words to Peter at the post-resurrection seaside meeting mirrored the words of his first call to Peter: "You [must] follow me" (John 21:22). Peter later wrote to other elders in the church to remind them of the ultimate reward: "When the chief Shepherd appears, you will receive the unfading crown of glory" (1 Peter 5:4).

USER GUIDE

YOUR MOTIVATION

TAKE A PERSONAL retreat of at least a day and write your "story" with a view toward fanning the flame of your love for Christ. Recount your personal testimony of how you came to faith in Jesus Christ. Who were the people God used in your life? What were the circumstances? If you have time, describe how God called you to gospel ministry. Read your testimony to your family, share it with your church staff, and, if you have opportunity, share it at a men's breakfast or a church-wide event.

In order to accomplish this, be sure to find a place where you will not be interrupted. In many regions there are camps and facilities that allow access to a quiet place you can use for a day or two.

For Further Reflection

1. How motivated are you to shepherd the flock? What is your motivation?
2. According to what we see in John 21, what is the right motivation for shepherding the flock?

3. What factors does the first chapter say may contribute to dampening a shepherd's motivation? Can you think of others?
4. Take a few moments to remember and be thankful for the grace God showed you (a) when he called you to faith and (b) when he called you to serve as a leader.
5. Have you wandered? Hear Jesus's call to repent and be restored, then identify the way home. Is there someone you can ask to come alongside you to provide counsel and support?

PART 1

SHAPING A SHEPHERDING STRUCTURE

2

FOUR PRINCIPLES FOR AN EFFECTIVE SHEPHERDING STRUCTURE

KEN JONES

SHEPHERDING IS MINISTERING to the whole person—physically, emotionally, spiritually, and relationally—so that all are equipped to follow God's call for their lives. Every church faces the hard question of how to provide wise, supportive, and effective shepherding care. In order to best accomplish this care, a church's leaders must build a strong and sustainable shepherding structure that will last for decades. These structures will vary from church to church and need to be fine-tuned over the years.

The church I serve as shepherding pastor, Oak Mountain Presbyterian (OMPC), has 2,800 members.[1] With so many in our care, we invested heavily in making sure our church's shepherding structure would promote God's glory and the good of

---

1. Note: Between this chapter's writing and its publication, I became senior pastor of Amelia Plantation Chapel on Amelia Island, Florida.

others. We wanted our leaders to value shepherding as Jesus valued it. Since Christ shed his precious blood for the church (Acts 20:28), we urged our leaders to share their time to care for the fold.

OMPC has eight shepherding teams that are made up of about 140 people in total. Led by a resource pastor who is a member of the staff at OMPC, each team is comprised of shepherding elders, elder trainees, and members of the women's shepherding team.[2] If a shepherding team is addressing a crisis in the congregation, a deacon joins the team to provide wisdom and input.

We employ an intentional structure that is built around the principles of commitment, encouragement, accountability, and equipping, especially for crisis response. The rest of this chapter unpacks these principles.

Commitment

The first principle of a healthy shepherding structure is that its leaders must be *committed*. Without commitment, any shepherding ministry is doomed to fail. In the context of shepherding, to be committed is to be joined in a fellowship that is entrusted with a sacred mission. With this in mind, OMPC penned a comprehensive shepherding code of ethics, shepherding vows, and a clear shepherd position description in order to ensure the highest standards of safety, security, and pastoral care for our flock. These documents promote commitment to the sacred mission by reinforcing the

---

2. The women's shepherding team offers wisdom to the elders in the ethos of Philippians 4:3, which tells us *to labor side by side in the gospel*. Sue Harris, OMPC's women's ministry director and my former colleague, has written a helpful chapter in this book (chapter 7) on women's shepherding teams in which she provides more details.

shepherd's high calling,[3] promoting lifelong learning, and encouraging fellowship with other shepherds of the congregation.

Every year, our elders vow to "shepherd out of love for God and His people" and to "pray diligently for the church, the families [they] are shepherding, and the work of [their] Shepherding team." With these public vows, our shepherds take responsibility for personally knowing their sheep. Their annual renewal of these vows produces a deeper commitment for the assigned fold.

What does this commitment look like? OMPC places each of its members' households under the care of a shepherding elder who periodically checks in with them.[4] Because our members are regularly contacted by church leadership in a relationally authentic way, our large church functions like a smaller family unit in which everyone is seen, known, and connected. By making regular, proactive contact with their sheep, our shepherds build relational credibility and establish a personal lifeline of care that members can draw on for help in their time of need.[5]

---

3. In the words of our code of ethics, "[Shepherds of God's flock] are responsible to God the Father, under Jesus Christ, by the power of His Spirit, to lead the congregation into the green pastures of God's Word that leads to true worship of Him."

4. This breaks down to about ten to twelve households per elder.

5. For a first-time contact, we suggest a shepherd say, "Hello, this is _____. I am an elder at OMPC. We desire for each family to have an official and close connection to our church officers, and I will be yours. What will that look like? It simply means I will be checking in on you and your family on an ongoing basis to see how you are doing. Please don't hesitate to reach out to me if you start to experience a situation where you need prayer and support." A good close to the conversation might sound like "I appreciate your willingness to talk to me and keep me updated. God's grace to you. Do you mind if I close our conversation with a prayer for you and your family?"

When we first implemented these shepherding contacts, one member summed it up best: "I appreciate you checking in. Never had that in the past, and it feels good to know that the body of Christ looks after each other."

Shepherding elders are responsible for responding to crisis situations within the households in their care, such as by organizing prayer ministry for the sick, making hospital visits, assisting with church discipline, and notifying pastoral staff of any pressing needs they discover. They commit to attending monthly officer meetings in which they report on the people in their fold. They are also charged to abide by the shepherding code of ethics, agreeing to "[ensure] that the glory of God and the best interest of the church member is achieved by complying with professionally accepted pastoral care practices (2 Corinthians 8:21) that exalt the name of Christ, our Chief Shepherd (1 Peter 5:1–5)."

Encouragement and Accountability

Although our church has set up clear expectations for elders, we seek to ensure fruitful shepherding not through a command-and-control approach to accountability but through collaboration and celebration. This comes primarily through our monthly shepherding leadership dinners—joyous evenings of dialogue amongst our leadership teams. These dinners have encouraged leaders and their shepherding teams to faithfully contact and connect with their sheep for the cause of Christ.

What does this look like? Each month, our shepherding leaders attend a large group meeting, then break into their individual shepherding teams to report on their current ministry endeavors with their fold and to seek the fellowship, collaboration, and wisdom of the other leaders.

We developed a format based on seven *I* words for this monthly gathering. We start with a prayer of *invocation* and then enjoy a high-energy *inter-relational* dinner with lively conversations. From there we engage in relevant *information* sharing and an *inspiration* time of vision-casting from the Scriptures, usually led by our senior pastor. At that time, we may also sing worship songs together. We then enter into a substantial time of *intercessory* prayer for the world and our congregation. Next comes *instruction,* as one of our pastoral staff members equips us with skills for being better shepherds (Eph. 4:11–12). Finally, for about an hour we break into our separate shepherding teams for *implementation*— doing the work of making shepherding plans and coordinating crisis responses. These small-group meetings close with further intercessory prayer for our members and communities.[6]

The *implementation* portion of our monthly dinners is one of the important ways we achieve accountability. During this time, we shepherd the shepherds by asking them to share the state of their hearts. Some of the most tender moments in pastoral care come as shepherds love on fellow shepherds who are struggling. When shepherds extend such gracious concern to one another, it only enhances the mission.

During implementation, we also encourage team members to ask one another for insights on how to best shepherd the people in their fold. We believe strongly in mutual aid. We tell our leaders, "If you feel like you're shepherding alone, then you're doing it wrong." In law enforcement, one officer is backed up by another at the scene of crisis, and the Bible says that a threefold cord is not quickly broken (Eccl. 4:12). Jesus said to minister two-by-two (Luke 10:1), so we use our monthly dinners to make sure that shepherds are not ministering in silos but are being engaged and supported by other shepherds.

When shepherding team members *connect* regularly with one another, they are consistently encouraged to *contact* the members

---

6. We very intentionally placed prayer at the beginning, middle, and end of the evening.

of the congregation. In situations that need extra attention, the shepherding team members *collaborate* with one another, asking the Holy Spirit to give them the wisdom to best *care* for our church family.

These four Cs of shepherding lead to a fifth: *celebration*. Timothy Witmer writes, "Expect to be encouraged as you see the Good Shepherd at work *in* you as you rely on his grace and wisdom to minister to the flock."[7] During our monthly dinners, we celebrate the ministry stories that are generated by the faithful shepherding of the congregation. It's encouraging to hear how God has met the needs of his people through timely contacts by his shepherds. Shepherds have supported members who were going through major surgeries or illnesses or coached congregants in their career callings. They have intervened with individuals who were quietly struggling with depression, anxiety, panic attacks, marital or family discord, financial distress, or suicidal thoughts. In one dramatic story, one of our shepherds went to a house to secure a loaded gun so that no one was accidently hurt. Sometimes a conversation with a shepherd is all it takes for a member who is not attending worship to make the commitment to regularly participate. These stories remind us that "blessed are the peacemakers who help others into the peace of God that is in Jesus Christ."[8]

Equipping for Crisis

Our shepherding structure was built for crisis. Much of shepherding is about crisis response, and to respond well requires

7. Timothy Z. Witmer, *The Shepherd Leader: Achieving Effective Shepherding in Your Church* (Phillipsburg, NJ: P&R Publishing, 2010), 249.

8. David Powlison, *Seeing with New Eyes: Counseling and the Human Condition through the Lens of Scripture* (Phillipsburg, NJ: P&R Publishing, 20030, 199.

much training and equipping. A truly prepared shepherd must have the integrity and skills to be a competent first responder (or, better, a *shepherd responder*) to those in desperate need. A shepherd must be like King David, who "with upright heart . . . shepherded them and guided them with his skillful hand" (Ps. 78:72).

Our shepherd leaders receive ongoing, monthly training to prepare them for the situations they will face. The topics of instruction have ranged from coaching, hospital visitations, and grief care to the impact of ACEs (adverse childhood experiences), suicide intervention, and trauma-informed care. Like emergency dispatchers, shepherds must be able to refer people to appropriate places for help or deploy the resources of the church in order to respond to a member who needs extra care. We instruct them on how to conduct these types of conversations and move forward.

Research demonstrates that those who isolate from faith-based community may be in urgent distress, so proactive shepherding outreach is crucial. Church staff issue notifications to shepherds about missing families through weekly missing-in-action (MIA) reports. If households have missed three or four Sundays in a row, their shepherd elders must immediately report on the cause. Such ongoing absences are a sign of a potential crisis, and as the Puritans remind us, "Satan watcheth for those vessels that sail without a convoy."[9] The MIA reports identify shepherding care cases at the earliest possible point of need.[10]

---

9. I. D. E. Thomas, *A Puritan Golden Treasury* (Carlisle, PA: Banner of Truth, 1977), 77.

10. Between the monthly shepherding team meetings and the weekly MIA reports, we have established a highly functioning two-part shepherding structure. This combination provides a communication and follow-up feedback loop that ensures all members are contacted. Even if a leader misses a monthly meeting, he will still be notified if one of his sheep is in distress (MIA, bereaved, grieving, sick) so that he can provide caring follow-up.

It is mandatory for every member to know who their shepherding elder is so they can call him in an emergency, and when this happens, the shepherd must respond 100 percent of the time with Christlike concern. We continually ask, "Are the members of the shepherding teams proactively reaching out to the sheep, and do the sheep feel welcome to call out to their shepherds in a time of need?" In our minds, this is the best way to evaluate the efficacy of any shepherding structure.

Imagine coming home to find your house broken into by a burglar. Your valuables have been stolen and your home vandalized. You feel insecure and numb. Once you notified the police, and perhaps family and friends, who would you call? At OMPC, we hope your next call would be to your shepherd elder so that he could pray for you and spiritually support you. He would also let the church know. The shepherding pastor, deacons, and trained women of the shepherding team, with God's wisdom, would devise a response plan to support you through your struggle. Contemplate the blessing of knowing that a grace-driven team of elders, deacons, commissioned women, and a shepherding pastor has mobilized in Christ's name for the sole purpose of tailoring a loving response to your family's crisis—not just one Good Samaritan helping you but a *team* of Good Samaritans responding.

OMPC has established three levels of shepherding response to any situation as we tend "the flock of God that is among [us]" (1 Peter 5:2). The first level is for the shepherd to respond personally to the sheep's need with conversation and prayer. This empowers our church members. When additional input is needed, the shepherd moves to the second level: canvassing the shepherding team for additional wisdom on the situation. In the third level of response, the shepherd consults with the shepherding pastor. We instruct our shepherds to immediately report to the shepherding pastor any situation that falls under one of the five emergency *A*s: *abuse* (suicide, threats, harm), *addictions*, *adultery*, *abandonment* (marital separations), and *abnormal psychology*. In these and other level-three situations, the shepherding pastor steps in to organize crisis care, counseling, coaching, or church discipline as necessary. In this way, even the messiest cases receive a swift and Christ-centered response.

In the case of those who are suicidal, our shepherds are trained to listen to them and then encourage them by saying, "God always loves you, he will never forsake you,[11] and I want you to live. I'm on your side, and we'll get you through this. Will you go with me to get help from a counselor or pastor? Will you call the National Lifeline?" Some of our shepherds have used this training to walk struggling members to the shepherding pastor's office to receive pastoral care and counseling.

No matter who is moving in to help, we encourage our shepherds to "always make it clear that you are not what this person needs—God is."[12] We are only following the example of the One who says, "I myself will be the shepherd of my sheep, and I myself will make them lie down, declares the Lord God. I will seek the lost, and I will bring back the strayed, and I will bind up the injured, and I will strengthen the weak" (Ezek. 34:15–16).

A Test for Our Shepherding Structure

If there was ever a year when people could fall through the cracks, it was 2020. With this in mind, OMPC conducted a comprehensive shepherding sweep at the start of the pandemic,

---

11. See Hebrews 13:5.

12. Paul David Tripp, *Instruments in the Redeemer's Hands: People in Need of Change Helping People in Need of Change* (Phillipsburg, NJ: P&R Publishing, 2002), 157.

asking our shepherding team members to contact the entire church family in twenty-four hours in order to check on them. They did it!

The initial response was amazing. One member told us, "I am so thankful for our leadership taking care of the flock. Thankful for each of you!" Another wrote, "Thanks, shepherds, for loving our church so well!" Even those who didn't usually respond to shepherding calls got back into touch with members of the team. A shepherd thanked us for initiating the sweep and for equipping the teams with questions to ask.[13]

Many prayer requests came in as a result of this outreach. A couple of members reported financial concerns. They had been embarrassed to ask for help, but due to their shepherd's call, they were able to get assistance. Other members reported suicidal ideation, and their shepherds made sure they received care from a professional Christian counselor who was paid out of the church's mercy fund. We would not have known about these situations if we had not been proactive.

When crisis hit, OMPC had systems in place to care for those who were impacted. Our shepherding system was built for a crisis—even a pandemic. We responded quickly, especially when specific aid was needed, and provided spiritual reassurance to struggling people. As shepherds followed up with members of their flocks, they were able to bring down the temperature in many people's emotional lives. Ultimately, we were inspired by

---

13. We used *Spiritual First Aid*, a resource released by Wheaton College's Humanitarian Disaster Institute. See Jamie D. Aten, et al., *Spiritual First Aid* (Wheaton, IL: Humanitarian Disaster Institute), 2020. *Spiritual First Aid* suggests asking the following questions of people in crisis: Are they connecting to others? Do they have pressing financial needs? Are they experiencing personal distress? How is their relationship with Jesus going? Are they acting in a safe manner? We found this to be a helpful way to walk through the necessary issues we needed to address.

our Lord Jesus Christ, whose love compels us to shepherd more and more people in God's grace.

Conclusion

In order to be fruitful, every shepherding ministry must have a healthy structure. When we applied in a pastorally caring way the principles of *commitment, encouragement, accountability,* and *equipping,* particularly for crises, we built a strong and effective shepherding framework.

Although each church needs to fine-tune shepherding for its own context, we found that this structure enabled us, by the Lord's grace, to best follow Paul's honorable call to "pay careful attention to yourselves and to all the flock, in which the Holy Spirit has made you overseers, to care for the church of God, which he obtained with his own blood" (Acts 20:28).

USER GUIDE

YOUR COMMITMENT AND PREPARATION

Commitment

Dr. Jones notes that "every year, our elders vow to 'shepherd out of love for God and His people' and to 'pray diligently for the church, the families [they] are shepherding, and the work of [their] Shepherding team.' With these public vows, our shepherds take responsibility for personally knowing their sheep. Their annual renewal of these vows produces a deeper commitment for the assigned fold." This would be a good project for a leaders' retreat.

Take some time to discuss what this "commitment" looks like in your church. Are the commitments of an elder clearly outlined?

Crisis

Jones writes, "If there was ever a year when people could fall through the cracks, it was 2020. With this in mind, OMPC conducted a comprehensive shepherding sweep at the start of the pandemic, asking our shepherding team members to contact the entire church family in twenty-four hours in order to check on them. They did it!" This crisis proved the benefit of a proactive shepherding plan.

The importance of preparing and equipping for crisis is an emphasis of Jones's chapter. Macro crises (such as a pandemic) impact the whole church, while micro crises strike an individual or a family. Proactive, crisis-aware shepherding also proves to be useful during leadership transitions. Sadly, when a church is between pastors, members are prone to wander. During such periods, the lifeline between shepherds and their flocks is crucial. Regular, personal communication between elders and their sheep can alleviate the confusion and frustration that often arise during transitional times.

Crisis preparation is crucial for a church of any size. How prepared is your church? Set aside a time for the elders of your church to discuss what "crisis response" looks like in your church. Reflect on what went well and what didn't go so well in recent crises. If you are anticipating a pastoral transition, be sure that your shepherding plan is up-to-date and functioning. Consider what is necessary to equip elders for crisis scenarios. This would also be worth spending time on during a retreat.

For Further Reflection

1. Does your shepherding structure contain clear guidance regarding the shepherd elders' commitments and responsibilities? What, if anything, could you do to clarify these expectations?
2. Does your shepherding structure provide regular opportunities for your shepherds to be equipped and encouraged? Have you gained additional ideas from reading this chapter?

3. Are the shepherd leaders of your church proactively reaching out to the sheep? What has come out of this? How do you know whether the sheep of your church feel welcome to call out to their shepherds in a time of need?

3

Shepherding the Flock: A Ruling Elder's Perspective

Gary L. Smith

WHAT COMPELS ELDERS to develop and participate in an intentional shepherding ministry? For the elders at our church, our transition from overseeing to shepherding began with a season of study and prayer. In our session meetings, elders discussed their desire and need to better know and be known by our members—a desire to fulfill the shepherding role that is so well defined in the Scriptures. As our pastors led the way, we began to understand what Jesus's command to "feed my sheep" really meant, and the entire shepherding ministry formation team experienced a Spirit-driven change in mindset.

Ultimately, we have been blessed to participate in the creation of our church's shepherding ministry and, more importantly, to serve the members of our church in our role as shepherds.

A Shift in Focus

Central Presbyterian Church in St. Louis, Missouri, recently celebrated its 175th anniversary. With over 1,100 adult members and seven hundred households, our church has historically had a big front door. We have welcomed many people who have been strengthened and encouraged by our faithful preaching, Christ-centered worship, and various programs. However, like other large churches, Central has had a big back door as well. Those who were not quickly brought into fellowship tended to leave.

Central has multiple pastors on staff and a large session that has approached forty ruling elders in size. Over the years, we had tried to develop ministry programs that were focused on shepherding, but they had not been sustained. Our elders had a heart for shepherding, but, until recently, the church's session was largely administrative. Although some organic shepherding occurred, the session did not provide systematic, intentionally relational shepherding care to the entire church membership as a flock.

In 2017, the elders on Central's session recognized that we needed to focus on shepherding the flock and to spend less time on administrative issues. We asked ourselves, "How can we best serve and care for the long-term needs of our congregation?" A passage that shaped our conviction and guided our subsequent changes was 1 Peter 5:1–3:

> So I exhort the elders among you, as a fellow elder and a witness of the sufferings of Christ, as well as a partaker in the glory that is going to be revealed: shepherd the flock of God that is among you, exercising oversight, not under compulsion, but willingly, as God would have you; not for shameful gain, but eagerly; not domineering over those in your charge, but being examples to the flock.

As the session examined this passage, the elders became convinced that we were giving an inordinate amount of time and energy to exercising oversight and very little time and energy to personally shepherding the flock of God that was among us. We decided to correct course: the primary emphasis of our leadership would be on shepherding and relationships, and the exercise of oversight would take on a secondary role. This was a major shift in focus.

As we made this shift, our first goal was to make a large church feel smaller by creating intentional, long-term relationships with each member. We wanted to get to know each member better and care for them as the Scriptures have asked us to do.

The elders of Central knew we needed a system to shepherd Central's many members toward a deeper relationship with Jesus the Good Shepherd and his church. A congregational survey revealed that our members wanted to connect and interact more with the church leadership as well. The desires of the congregation and the session were together coming into alignment with God's will for his church.

Making the Change

To make the changes we desired, the session essentially needed to reinvent itself. Our first step was to set apart certain elders to focus on administration in order to free the rest to care for the flock. We created a governance commission of seven elders who would each serve for a set amount of time as they handled the session's administrative responsibilities.

Next, the session created a shepherding task force that had the responsibility of developing a new shepherding policy for Central. In turn, the task force created a new *flock oversight team* to implement, support, and sustain the shepherding ministry.[1] Together the shepherding task force and flock oversight team envisioned an ideal shepherding ministry, attempted to forecast any problems that would hinder its launch and long-term viability, and created workable solutions to those potential problems. During this process, we sought the counsel of similarly sized churches around the country that had established shepherding ministries. These churches shared programs, support documents, and ideas with us that greatly helped us as we prayerfully started and built our ministry.

The plan we developed was to launch and train shepherding teams that could better serve all members—both men and women—of the church. We divided Central's membership into over fifty "flocks" of approximately ten to fifteen households each, paying attention to geographical locations and educational districts that would enhance common bonds within the flock groups. Next we assigned each flock to a shepherding team that consisted of a ruling elder and one or more people in a new "lay shepherd" position that we created. We had wanted to find opportunities for women to be more involved in leadership, and this new lay shepherd position helped to serve that purpose. Thus we have established shepherd leadership teams that consist of both a male shepherd and a female shepherd.[2]

To secure unanimous buy-in among the members of session, we implemented a monthly study meeting in which we reviewed

---

1. The exact membership of the flock oversight team has varied over the years, but according to our governing policies it must be composed of the congregational care pastor, at least two ruling elders, and at least one woman. It currently consists of our pastor of congregational care, our director of women's ministry, three ruling elders, three female lay representatives from the congregation, and the executive assistant to the pastor of congregational care, who provides administrative support.

2. Many, but not all, of the shepherding teams are husband and wife teams.

and discussed the wording of the policies that would govern the session and the church as we moved forward. The session thus received the new governance model incrementally and adopted it in preliminary form. The process lasted about nine months and resulted in the new governance model's unanimous adoption when the time came for it to be approved in its entirety.

The flock oversight team launched the ministry in the fall of 2017, in cooperation and collaboration with the church's staff and other ministries. It had the full support of the senior pastor, congregational care pastor, additional pastors, and staff. Today this support is made known from the pulpit, frequently communicated to the congregation, and referred to in nearly every session meeting. Such support is important for the success and effectiveness of the ministry.

Our shepherding ministry overlays and encompasses the entire church membership and other church ministries in a relational, systematic, and process-driven fashion. Its intent and purpose are to ensure that all our shepherds pursue intentional, long-term personal relationships with their flock members in order to nurture their spiritual growth. We want the shepherds to know the members who have been assigned to their flocks and want the members to know their shepherds.

Our Guiding Principles

The four Cs of shepherding are the guiding principles for the shepherds of our church. They are the key themes and drivers for our shepherding ministry.

Contact. We ask each shepherd team to contact each member of their flock at least once every quarter. This contact should be intentional and consistent. We want our shepherd teams to speak to their members in person or to text them and receive a response. Most importantly, we ask our shepherds to ask for prayer requests and to pray with and for their members whenever they connect.

To advance and improve communications from the flock oversight team and the church leadership to our shepherd teams, we created a regular email contact tool called Shepherds' Staff Note. To help to track shepherd contacts with members, the flock oversight team created another tool called the Shepherd Flock Report. Each team's flock members are listed in a simple document spreadsheet, along with space to write notes or suggestions that the flock oversight team can view. It is easy for the shepherd teams to fill out the reports and for the flock oversight team to access and discuss them in our meetings. Using the tool, the shepherd teams prepare quarterly flock reports as a way of remaining accountable for successfully contacting their members.

Connection. Our shepherd teams should know each flock member well and help them to connect in a deeper way with God and his church. Our shepherds encourage members to participate actively in at least one ministry group so that they can connect to the church's community life. In our communications and in our training meetings, the flock oversight team keeps our shepherds informed of ministry events and opportunities so that shepherds can help their flock members to connect or serve more effectively. The shepherd teams also connect church members with acute needs to appropriate people and resources (such as pastors, counselors, and support groups) for more specialized care as their situations require.

Collaboration. The shepherding ministry overarches the entire church and links to and enhances all the church's other ministries.

One example is the collaboration between our shepherding ministry and our family ministry. If a child is struggling, our director of family ministries reaches out to their family's shepherding elder to encourage contact so that elder can pray for and come alongside that family.

Care. Shepherding care is expressed through prayer, service, and support. Prayer is a particular priority and a key imperative in the shepherding relationship. We encourage teams to ask for prayer requests and to pray with and for their flock members.

Training and Ongoing Development

When establishing a shepherding ministry, a church must consider the willingness of the shepherds to do the biblical and practical tasks they are called to do. As we got started, the flock oversight team, with the support of the church staff and our session, created a process to identify qualified ruling elders and lay shepherds who could serve on the shepherd teams. Our session policy required all active session members to have flocks, but we were grateful that many elders in the church who were no longer actively serving on the session were also eager to serve as shepherd elders. That same eagerness to serve was demonstrated by the lay shepherds whom we asked to join the teams. Now, when new elder candidates are selected and trained, we emphasize the role of shepherding before they are installed.

Since we started our program, we have trained over one hundred shepherds to support their flocks. We created a guide for them that details their role, ministry goals, and support resources. We also provide ongoing training for the shepherd teams, primarily through a quarterly all-shepherds' meeting that all the teams attend. These meetings begin with a short devotion and a time of fellowship over a meal. Because we believe it is essential for the success of this ministry for us to be fed and instructed by the Scriptures, empowered by the Spirit, and directed by the Bible, we normally begin the formal part of our meetings with exhortation from God's Word. After the biblical training, we recite the church's vision statement and have a formal program update and a talk from a featured speaker or trainer. We end the large-group time with prayer and break into small groups for (1) a personal "shepherd heart check," which allows our shepherds to care for one another, (2) a "flock check," in which the teams discuss how things are going with each flock, and (3) mutual prayer for the shepherd teams and their flocks. The small-group times provide encouragement and accountability among shepherd teams in a friendly environment with people who all are committed to this necessary work.

Although the shepherd teams meet together quarterly the flock oversight team, from its inception to today, has met almost weekly. This is necessary for the ministry's long-term sustainability. We also conduct an annual planning retreat to evaluate the ministry and set goals for the coming year.[3] This is a great opportunity for the flock oversight team to see where we need to improve and brainstorm ways forward. It's also a time for us to think outside the box about how we can make this ministry even more vibrant. And it's a time for us to enjoy fellowship together, which makes us a better team.

It is important to emphasize that Central's shepherding ministry is in continuous development as we seek to improve it.

3. We always begin by evaluating how we're doing using Timothy Witmer's "Seven Essential Elements of an Effective Shepherding Ministry," chap. 9 in *The Shepherd Leader: Achieving Effective Shepherding in Your Church* (Phillipsburg, NJ: P&R Publishing, 2010).

Keeping the flocks organized and the rolls accurate is an ongoing task as well. When new members join the church, they are assigned to a flock, and their shepherds connect with them immediately. When shepherd teams need to step down, as happens from time to time, their flocks are redistributed. The flock oversight team asks each shepherd team to go through their flock one name at a time, once a year, to gauge the health of the flock and to help it in any way they can.

Closing Thoughts

When Central's session realized that we needed to shift our focus, our shepherds overall were committed to the biblical role of elder. They focused on what they were called to do and were obedient to the Word. Yet being a *shepherd* was a mindset change for a number of our elders. The relationship between these elders and the members and lay shepherds was transformed as they connected intentionally, got to know one another, and prayed with and for one another. Hearts softened and became more open in this process.

How does this mindset shift? One elder said, "Elders must view the role as a biblical mandate and not as a church program." Other shepherds commented,

> There was the initial fear of being unqualified, unequipped to do the tasks, but that was overcome by the joy of connecting and the trust that developed with flock members.

> Being an elder is a true calling of the heart. From the start, I wanted the shepherd role versus the administrative role, as

elders are called to be shepherds first and foremost. Being a shepherd is a privilege . . . a biblical invitation to serve.

[To be a servant leader] is a humbling role with a need for deep humility.

[It] is such a blessing to get to know brothers and sisters as we have the opportunity as shepherds. I believe if everyone had the chance to experience what we get to experience, they all would sign up to be shepherds.

The congregation has come to see their elders as shepherds, not just administrators—a true transformation indeed.

The following comments reflect the relational experiences of flock members.

Trust was established through connection and prayer and was better than expected.

We are getting to know church members differently and discovering how to know and love them better.

Shepherding the flocks helped to create a sense of belonging and unity. It's demonstrable; you can see and feel it.

Based on feedback we have received, we believe our shepherd teams have made somewhere between 7,000 and 9,000 connections with members in the last four years. Our measurements indicate that in any given quarter we connect with over 60 percent of the membership and that 80 to 90 percent of those connections are covered in prayer. We believe those connections have a multiplying effect as contacted members share the conversations and prayers with the members of their households.

Our senior pastor believes that Central's shepherding ministry was the glue that helped to hold the church together during the COVID pandemic, especially when people deeply felt the isolating effects of sequestering. The shepherding ministry served as a shock absorber for the church as it helped members to communicate and connect. We believe we are praying more persistently as a church now and that deeper levels of trust exist between us all.

We are grateful to the Lord, our Good Shepherd, for guiding us in the way, the Word, and the truth so that we may then love, honor, obey, and serve him and love his people well.

USER GUIDE

RAISING UP ELDERS

Where do the elders come from? One of the biggest challenges that churches face is having enough *qualified* elders to effectively care for their members. Paul tells Pastor Timothy, "*Do not be too quick in the laying on of hands* and thereby share in the sins of others. Keep yourself pure" (1 Tim. 5:22 BSB). There is a great temptation to just "find someone" or to fill in the slots of the next "class" of elders.

How many elders should a church have? It should have as many as are called, gifted, and qualified to be elders. No more. No less.

Someone asked Timothy Witmer what he would have done differently as he looked back on his decades of ministry. His answer was "I would have spent more time investing in the men of the church."

Spend some time considering how men are discipled in your church. Reflect on how current elders were raised up. Was there a process, or did it "just happen"? Identify a plan for thoughtfully and deliberately preparing future officers.

For Further Reflection

1. Why form a shepherding ministry? Why form one at your church? Why do it now?
2. When you think of "shepherding," what elements of that role come to your mind?
3. As you consider the ideas presented in chapter 3, what ought you to pray for in your own church?
4. Think of someone in your church who you think would make an effective shepherd. What would help that person to succeed?
5. What mindset barriers to shepherding do you need to address among your elders?
6. How have you seen God move in your life, or in the lives of the members of your flock, as you have participated in shepherding ministry?

4

SHEPHERDING EVERY MEMBER,
MEETING EVERY NEED

JOHN BARRETT

IN THE EARLY 1800s, First Presbyterian Church in Augusta, Georgia, grew to two hundred fifty members. At this time, the leadership instructed each elder "to watch over the spiritual interests of the people of the congregation, to visit and pray with the sick, comfort the afflicted and distressed, relieve the wants of the poor, take cognizance of any cases requiring discipline, see that the children attend Sunday school, and discharge all other duties devolving upon the overseers of Christ."

This very plan guided my predecessor at this church, Rev. Robert Irvine, during his pastorate in the 1870s. During his ten years of ministry at First Presbyterian, nearly four hundred new members joined the church. The elders regularly dealt with matters in the congregation involving drunkenness, the sale of "ardent spirits," absence from worship services, the conducting of business on Sunday, profanity, quarreling, malicious gossip, worldly amusement (such as dancing, gambling, and card playing), dishonesty in business, dueling, and an issue that had long perplexed Presbyterians: the marriage of a member to the widow of a deceased brother.

Although some of these problems were unique to their time, others are perennial in the life of the church and will always need spiritual oversight. In the days of old under the ministry of Irvine, our church delegated this oversight to elders by geographic areas. Their efforts were imperfect. They were often misunderstood and at times were characterized as heavy-handed, while at other times they were seen as laissez-faire. Yet they continued to implement this plan in spite of these accusations.

On April 8, 1881, the Reverend Robert Irvine was buried in the shadow of the sanctuary of our church. He had faithfully pastored First Presbyterian for the last ten years of his life, and the small congregation wanted to honor him in his death. They commissioned a life-size statue of Irvine and placed it on a marble pedestal that measures over twenty feet high. Etched on the west side of his monument are the following words: "Above all, a man who, like his Master, went about doing good. A man of character abounding and of tender heart. The poor, the sick, and the sorrowing found in him a friend whose counsel, sympathy, and aid were at their command." Simply stated, Irvine's legacy, etched in stone, is that he gave himself to the shepherding of his flock.

In this chapter, I will discuss how our church defined an ideal and systematic shepherding plan in the years following Irvine, the challenges we faced in implementing this plan, and some of the solutions we discovered along the way.

The Ideal Shepherding Plan

The ideal shepherding plan must be biblical above all. At First Presbyterian, the two verses that have most shaped our shepherding plan are Acts 20:28 and 1 Peter 5:2. Two phrases within these verses have guided our thoughts and efforts.

The first phrase comes from Paul's words to the Ephesian elders: "Pay careful attention to yourselves and to *all the flock*, in which the Holy Spirit has made you overseers, to care for the church of God, which he obtained with his own blood" (Acts 20:28). This verse sets the *scope* of our shepherding plan. We are not required to know *some* of our flock or even *most* of our flock. Rather, we are called to know *all* our flock. This means that the starting point for our church's shepherding plan must include a systematic way for us to shepherd *all* the flock.

The second phrase comes from 1 Peter: "Shepherd the flock of God that is among you, *exercising oversight*, not under compulsion, but willingly, as God would have you; not for shameful gain, but eagerly" (1 Peter 5:2). *Exercising oversight* in this context means paying careful attention to the needs of the sheep and then willingly, eagerly, and sacrificially moving toward those under your care. This addresses the *depth* of shepherding ministry.

Guided by these two principles, our leadership adopted the aspirational goal that we will *know every member of our church and care for every need within the church.* Is this idealistic? Yes. Believe me, many within our leadership have wanted to modify this profound statement because it is not just idealistic but unrealistic. Yet the measure of the statement is not whether or not it is realistic or idealistic but whether or not it is biblical. We believe it is, and so as a church we set out to build a plan that had in its sight the goal of shepherding every member of the church and meeting every need within the church.

Shepherding 1.0

One of the first questions shepherding leaders must ask themselves as they build an effective shepherding plan is how they intend to organize themselves and their charges. They might do so by geographical areas, small groups, fellowship groups, or elder "draft" selection.[1] While it does not matter which criterion you select, once you select one you must tenaciously stay with it, while being willing to make adjustments along the way.

Although First Presbyterian has gone through different iterations of its care plan since the early days described at the opening of this chapter, twenty years ago our leadership decided to double our efforts by organizing our care into parishes. I will call this initiative *Shepherding 1.0.* We redrew parish boundary lines, named the seventeen resulting parishes, developed a leadership structure, clarified our expectations for how often shepherds were to contact members, and included a plan of accountability in the event that elders were not making the needed contacts. After reading *The Shepherd Leader* and discussing it as a session, we agreed upon the following plan:

- We ensured that each parish had one parish elder.
- We created a team of under-shepherds in each parish to assist the elder.
- We assigned each elder and his under-shepherds between eight and ten households to oversee.
- We tasked each elder and under-shepherd to contact each member of their parish at least once every eight weeks.

1. See Timothy Z. Witmer, *The Shepherd Leader: Achieving Effective Shepherding in Your Church* (Phillipsburg, NJ: P&R Publishing, 2010), 204–8.

- We scheduled quarterly meetings with the elders to discuss the health of each parish.

This was our starting point. Although we knew there would be some additional areas to address, we had no idea just how many problems we were about to encounter related to this initiative.

Problems with Shepherding 1.0

Administration Problems

Multiple databases. At the heart of a systematic shepherding plan is an accurate roll. In our Shepherding 1.0 plan, we methodically confirmed each and every member's address, assigned shepherds to their respective parishes, and then began making contacts. About the time we finished this task, we realized that these assignments needed to be changed because many of our members had either moved within the city or moved beyond the city. To make matters worse, we were tracking changes of address and shepherding assignments through separate databases. It was not uncommon to have one household in our system under two addresses and therefore in two parishes without either elder knowing whether the family was in his flock.

Coordination between elders. The other administrative challenge was coordinating efforts between leaders. We encouraged elders and under-shepherds to share their shepherding logs with one another so they would know who had and had not been contacted within a parish. While our elders gave a noble effort, it was almost impossible for them to stay in touch with their flock members, document this contact on a computer, and share this information with another leader. This is because we used paper shepherding logs, a clunky database that could be used only on a computer, and our mobile phones. Our shepherding efforts folded under this administrative load. One kind elder told me, "I read the news on my phone, I bank on my phone, I check my email on my phone, and we need to build a shepherding plan that uses our phones." We all agreed, but we simply did not know how this could be possible.

Leadership Problems

Meeting schedule. Elders in the church were required to attend a monthly meeting. This meeting took place on the fourth Tuesday of the month. Under Shepherding 1.0 we had thirty elders, and most of our meetings were spent discussing the needed *business* of the church while giving little attention to the *shepherding* of the church. In order to create time for shepherding, we added another meeting to the schedule. This shepherding meeting was supposed to take place every other month and to involve not only the elders but also the under-shepherds. We tried different times and days and frequencies, but this meeting was difficult to fit into the rhythm of the church calendar and, more importantly, into the rhythm of the busy lives of those on our shepherding teams. Both the shepherding meeting and shepherding itself became low priorities, and commitment to the meeting waned after several years.

Inadequate number of elders. Additionally, we realized that we did not have enough elders. At the beginning of our shepherding initiative, we had thirty elders—and a membership of 1,800. We did not know what the ideal ratio would be, but after talking with other churches we recognized our numbers were low. A ratio of sixty members to each elder was not practical.

Discouraged elders. Finally, I would say that in these early days many of our elders were discouraged by the lack of response from members. Yes, there were many wonderful stories of elders contacting members and providing care, but many elders were disappointed because their flock members were not returning their calls. We worked hard to champion the small victories, but an undertow of cynicism began to pull this plan into the sea of despair.

Comprehensive Care Problems

As we built this Shepherding 1.0 plan, we thought of the various types of care that we would need to provide to meet every need. We outlined them as follows:

- *Continuous care.* This describes the bimonthly contact that all members of the flock receive from their elders and under-shepherds.
- *Common care.* This describes the care that members need in the event of a hospitalization or the birth of a child. It includes setting up a meal schedule and working with the deacons to take care of any practical jobs around the house that need to be done.
- *Crisis care.* This is care provided in the event of a tragic accident or sudden loss. In such times, a system of care can lose its credibility if it does not facilitate a compassionate and expeditious response.
- *Chronic care.* This is the type of care that often follows a crisis. It is the type of care that is often the most difficult. It is one thing to be there for a member at the onset of a crisis; it is another to be there for them a year later as they still grieve their loss.

- *Counseling care.* This is counseling done by a professional to engage with needs that require more specialized training to address well.

Although we had outlined the types of care we needed to be able to provide, we had not recruited our leaders for this purpose or trained them on how to respond when confronted with these various needs. As we slowly but surely improved our ability to provide continuous care, we were confronted with more and more members who needed help. Some of the help was needed only temporarily, which could be managed, but other times it was much more acute and needed ongoing focused attention. Some of our elders lamented that we could focus on either continuous care or crisis care but not both.

An example of this came when a husband was discovered to have committed adultery. The couple's parish elder was forced into a season of crisis care, which eventually transitioned into both chronic and counseling care. This was a two-year process, and in the end, by God's grace, the couple was restored. Afterward, however, the elder requested a year's sabbatical and acknowledged that he was able to give this type of attention to one couple only at the cost of the rest of his parish. He asked, "Am I to care for my whole flock [continuous care] or to care for the one member in trouble [crisis care]?" It was a great question, and while we all felt his burden, none of us had a satisfactory answer.

Solutions We Discovered (Shepherding 2.0)

We worked very hard to solve the problems of Shepherding 1.0, and what resulted from this essentially has become our Shepherding 2.0. Here are the solutions we have sought to apply.

Administration Solutions

A new database. There is a "ministry" side of the church and an "operations" side of the church. This can be a challenge. Each side is needed, but each has different requirements. An example of this is a church database. A church's operations side needs a database that can manage money. The ministry side of the church needs a database that can equip people. It has been said that most databases can manage either nickels or noses but few can do both.

This was certainly the case for our church. We were using a database that had been chosen over twenty years prior for its accounting features. The software company continued to make advancements in its financial suite without making the same strides on the ministry side. For example, if we wanted to know how many of our members were currently serving in the church or if we wanted to keep track of attendance on a Sunday morning, we had to use a separate system.

We knew databases out there promised to do both, but in order to make a change of such magnitude we needed to secure agreement among all the stakeholders. To the credit of our financial office and operations team, they allowed us to begin to explore other options, and eventually our church staff began a yearlong process of transitioning to a database that had been built with people and shepherding in mind. It was painful, but in the end we were left with a platform that not only managed the money but also allowed us to shepherd our people in ways we never could have imagined. The new system immediately addressed the challenges of inaccurate rolls and parish assignments.[2] When people changed addresses, they were automatically moved from their old parishes to their new parishes, and both parishes' sets

2. We are currently using MinistryPlatform (www.ministryplatform.com).

of elders were contacted so that a decision could be made as to their oversight. Although this may seem like a simple achievement, overnight it detangled dozens of perennial knots in our plan.

A custom-designed app. The new database provided a way for us to build a user-friendly app to coordinate our shepherding efforts. Such an app was first introduced to me by my shepherding mentor and friend Randy Schlichting.[3] When he demonstrated how it worked, I nearly broke into the Doxology. His church was using an app to create a user-friendly interface that indicated when each church member had last been contacted, measured their engagement based on a set of activity criteria, and allowed the elders to share a common shepherding log for each member. I had not known this was possible.

I asked Randy how they built this app, and to my amazement and joy it turned out to be possible because they were using the very database to which we had just transitioned! I nearly cried. At last our church was within striking distance of accomplishing just what our elder desired: the ability to use our phones to evaluate, communicate, indicate, and collaborate all our shepherding efforts on a common app. Did I think it would resolve all our shepherding challenges? No. Did I think it would be a quantum step forward? Yes, and three years later both conclusions have proven to be true.

Leadership Solutions

Refocus officers' meetings. Another change we made was to our officer meetings. We recognized that we could no longer

---

3. Randy is the author of chapter 5, "*Knowing* Every Member (with a Technological Assist)."

add meetings to the lives of our elders. We had a meeting once a month, and we needed to make it count. If shepherding is the essence of our elders' work, then the primary business we must attend to is the care of our members.

We spent a year discussing potential changes, and in the end we transitioned away from holding ten business meetings a year to now holding four business meetings and six care meetings. During these meetings, we provide continued shepherding training, separate into parish breakout groups to discuss and pray through ongoing issues with our members, and hold one another accountable for making our needed contacts. Each parish elder is provided with metrics on the number of contacts he has made and an overview of the activity levels of each member.

In order to make this shift, we had to commission a smaller body of elders to make certain decisions that the larger body had historically made. It has not come without a struggle. This has required a high level of trust within the leadership, but we concluded that if we were ever to shepherd effectively, we would have to delegate certain decisions to a smaller body in order to free ourselves to shepherd.

Another problem was partially resolved when we began to meet in smaller parish breakout gatherings during care meetings. Elders expressed their discouragement with the lack of response they were receiving from members, and we began to shepherd one another through this disappointment. Not only were we shepherding the flock under our care, we began shepherding one another. This was a hidden blessing in these meetings, and it has already proven to be of lasting value. In fact, we now dedicate a portion of our time just to check in with one another. It is clunky and awkwardly quiet at times, but we are learning that the best way to shepherd a flock is to remember that you are a part of it and need to be shepherded yourself.

Increase the number of elders and involve others. The final leadership challenge we faced was the inadequate number of elders. After considerable deliberation, we addressed this in two ways.

First, we built what we called a *leadership pipeline.* We hoped to identify men who aspired to the office of elder and then use the pipeline to provide a pathway for them to become officers in the church.

Second, we assigned families not only to the elders of our church but also to the deacons. In our form of governance, elders and deacons are distinct offices, but their differences did not exclude the deacons from participating in the parishes' shepherding assignments. We have also expanded our shepherding coverage by training qualified women to become part of the care team within each parish.[4] The women of our church are already informally caring for one another, so we thought it wise to both formalize their efforts and align them to our goal of shepherding the entire flock.

Comprehensive Care Solutions

Care teams. Our most difficult challenge is to build a shepherding system that meets every need within the church. We still have a long way to go, but we have made some progress by building auxiliary care systems to supplement each parish's care. In other words, we communicate to each parish elder that his primary job is to oversee the continuous care within his parish. We are working to build specialized teams and offer specialized services for when crisis or counseling needs present themselves. This requires additional leadership to identify members who can help to lead

---

4. See chapter 7, "Women Caring for Women in Support of Your Shepherding Ministry," by Sue Harris.

these initiatives. It may require supporting a counseling ministry within your church to address certain challenges. Even if these additional options are available, it requires a great deal of communication, prayerful consideration, and careful collaboration.

Support groups and process groups. Our church has been working to establish small groups that can help people to recover from life-dominating sins, addiction, or traumatic life events. Support groups provide encouragement and support during prolonged periods of suffering or hardship. Process groups help people to process problematic emotions or multiple life stressors. These groups are places we provide for deeper needs to be addressed without pulling a parish elder away from overseeing the breadth of his parish.

Shepherding 3.0?

I must now provide a disclaimer. Although I have answered each of these challenges with a subsequent solution, the reality is that all the solutions are in progress and are showing varying degrees of effectiveness. These solutions are being tested in the crucible of the church, and I am sure some will evolve and others will devolve. We have had to learn to live with a certain level of uncertainty and disappointment and with an incomplete plan. The truth of the matter is that there is no such thing as a perfect shepherding plan, and there never will be. Our systematic plan is riddled with problems. I pray that our current plan has less problems or at least different problems than our previous plan, but time will tell.

If you are committed to shepherding God's precious sheep, you must humbly join the rest of us and acknowledge that shepherding is a process, and in this process you must perseere if you are to experience the rewards. Whether you are on shepherding 1.0, 2.0, or 6.0, the key is to keep on keeping on for the glory of God and for the wellbeing of his flock.

Conclusion

In the final days of his ministry, Rev. Robert Irvine was diagnosed with bone fever. His doctor gave him strict orders to rest. Then news came to him that a certain widow of his congregation was nearing the end of her life. Irvine had promised this dear saint that he would hold her hand as she passed through the valley of the shadow of death. Against his doctor's orders and his better judgment, he sat with her through the night, praying with her and reading Scripture to her as she drifted into eternal sleep. It was his final act of ministry—he himself died a few weeks later.

Each time I walk past Irvine's statue on our campus, I am reminded of the high calling of those who shepherd the Lord's flock. It is a call to shepherd *all* the flock. It is a call to meet every need within the flock. It comes with challenges and disappointments, and when they arise I pray that the Lord gives me the strength to persevere in holding the hands of others, even at great cost to myself, knowing that the Good Shepherd is holding my hand both in this life and into the one to come.

USER GUIDE

THE PAST

REFLECTING ON THE exemplary shepherding care that Puritan pastor Richard Baxter provided for the thousand families who attended his parish, J. I. Packer writes, "How to do this today would have to be worked out in terms of present circumstances, which are very different from those Baxter knew and describes; but Baxter's question to us is, should we not be attempting this, as a practice constantly necessary? If he convinces us that we should, it will not be beyond us to find a method of doing it that suits our situation; where there's a will, there's a way."[1]

Take some time to outline the history of the shepherding ministry in your church. How many iterations do you remember? Why did they falter? Be objective as you analyze what's happening now and how you can improve as you move forward.

Remember—where there's a will, there's a way!

---

1. J. I. Packer, introduction to *The Reformed Pastor* by Richard Baxter (repr., Edinburgh: Banner of Truth, 1997), 19.

For Further Reflection

1. What factors have frustrated your efforts to shepherd the flock in the past?
2. Would you say that you are at shepherding 1.0, 2.0, or 0.0?
3. Are you convinced that shepherding is important to address? What steps could you take to reinvigorate your church's efforts to do so?
4. Whom might you contact to assist and encourage you as you move your shepherding ministry forward?

PART 2

SHEPHERDING EVERY MEMBER

5

KNOWING EVERY
MEMBER (WITH A
TECHNOLOGICAL ASSIST)

RANDY SCHLICHTING

The Problem

Each Sunday people shuffle into church, grab a seat, participate in worship, perhaps talk to a few other people, and then
leave, hopefully to return in seven days. Sadly, the average church-
goer does not. Perhaps they come twice a month. They are "on
site" for just three hours out of the seven hundred and twenty
hours in a month, and most of that time they are listening to
one person talk.

Some people engage with the church a bit more. They want
to do something during the week. They want to be in a small
group, possibly run by leaders in the church. They see the bene-
fits of being with other believers, and so they may spend two
hours or so during the week with other people from the church.

Some people want more. They want to belong. They want to join the church. Some of them are aware of the responsibilities and privileges of being a member of a church. In many churches, people actually go through some sort of membership class, complete a form, and share their spiritual testimony with someone in the church. At some point, someone in leadership says, "We are confirming that you are a Christian, and we welcome you into membership."

But what happens, or does not happen, *after* such a person joins the church? In many churches, the newcomer gets a welcome letter, giving envelopes, and a list of ministries in which they can serve or connect. They may get a call from someone in the church inviting them to participate in a group or to engage in service. It seems to work well on paper: new person joins the church, they get connected, and they live in the church happily ever after.

The church is called to admit those who are in Christ to membership *so that* they can be shepherded. The work of the church is not just to *admit* the saints but to *equip* the saints (Eph. 4:11–13). The apostle Paul called elders in the church to "keep watch over yourselves and all the flock of which the Holy Spirit has made you overseers" (Acts 20:28 NIV). But today many people are *not* members of a church, and many leaders do not know the people who are—they may know their names, but they don't know their spiritual condition. To know someone's spiritual condition, a leader must have a relationship with them, and that takes time: time on the phone, time by text, and time face-to-face to build trust, to listen, and to discern needs. Shepherds must *know* and *care* for the sheep the Lord has entrusted to them.

What we are talking about here is radical. We are talking about leaders knowing *all* the members of their churches and shepherding them regularly at the heart, hand, and head level. That type of shepherding takes diligence, prayer, and a system that works to promote accountability, encouragement, and insight for all.

The Solution

Perimeter Church has more than 4,500 members. In addition, we have about 1,500 regular attenders and a bunch of kids!

We don't have the same 4,500 members from year to year. About five hundred people leave each year and five hundred more arrive. We are blessed to see some people come to faith every year and join the church by profession. The rest of the new people come through transfer from another church or through reaffirmation of faith. Why do people leave? Some die. Some move. Some leave because the increasingly wicked traffic patterns in Atlanta make it too difficult for them to stay engaged. And, full disclosure, some leave because they disagree with our theology or ministry plan. But at the end of each year we have around 4,500 members, and about five hundred of them are new. That is a lot of "moving sheep" to shepherd.

About ten years ago, the Lord pressed upon our hearts the realization that we were not shepherding the sheep because we did not know them. We had admitted them to membership and the Lord's Supper, but we had not connected them to elders.

We began to ask some questions. "If every family had an elder, how many elders would this take?" "How many families could one elder shepherd?" "What would it mean to shepherd?" "How would we know we were shepherding?" As we asked these questions, Acts 20:28 kept gnawing at us: "Keep watch over yourselves and all the flock of which the Holy Spirit has made you overseers. Be shepherds of the church of God, which he bought with his own blood" (NIV). The Scriptures teach that elders are to keep watch over everyone who is a member of the flock. At Perimeter, we would say that means those who have joined the church, and are communing members, as well as their noncommuning offspring. God wants us to shepherd those whom he has bought with his blood, but we were convicted that we were not doing that and we had to find a better way.

Our first step was to check our math. With two hundred elders and about 2,300 households in our congregation, each elder would have to shepherd twelve households. That seemed like a lot. Our elders were primarily men who had families and worked in the marketplace. We could not task them with spending ten hours a week shepherding people. And we could not relationally overload them. We knew we needed more elders but did not want to lay hands on a man before he was called and ready. The bottom line was we had too many people and not enough elders.

When we started working out which families we might assign to each elder, the results were mixed. On the one hand, the elders did already know people in the church. On the other hand, they often lived a long way from the people they knew, meaning their possibility of connecting with them was small. We wanted to move to a parish (geographical) model for ministry. We wanted elders to live close to the people they shepherded, perhaps even in the same neighborhood with their children attending the same school. So it was messy.

As we were thinking about it, we added another question to the mix: "Do people *want* to be shepherded?" We could set up a system—we could "build it,"—but they might not come. In the Lord's graciousness, he reminded us that if we set up a system, new people would enter into it as part of the membership process. Remember, we see about a 20 percent turnover every year. So, if we set up a system and new people entered into that system as they became members, they would knowingly agree to be shepherded.

Problem solved . . . except we did not have enough elders, and the church leadership had not yet told them that they would each be taking on a new role that had not been part of their training. We had to define what it meant to shepherd, and we had to set up a system to help elders to do the work they were being called to do.

Shepherding Defined

How do you define *shepherding*? Perimeter defines it as overseeing the spiritual lives of members, and member families, in a holistic way. It should not be confused with *discipleship*, which is more involved in the day-to-day growth cycle of those members. The discipler works with individual members from week to week to massage the truth into their lives, to equip them, and to play an active role in their accountability. A shepherd does different work over a larger area.

The shepherd speaks truth into the lives of members. He makes sure members know where to get equipped. He exhorts them to have real accountability. He calls them to be missional and points them to opportunities to get engaged. He prays for them, asks them good questions, and encourages them to learn how to make supplication to the Lord.

The shepherd herds and watches. He inspects the sheep for signs of health. He is ready in a crisis. He discerns the lay of the land and determines whether there are storm clouds on the horizon. He looks, with other shepherds, at the condition of the land and for opportunities for mercy and justice to break forth in it.

Shepherds must be men of prayer. At Perimeter, we wanted our elders to ask God to do a work in and through them. We wanted them to ask the Holy Spirit to reveal whatever needed to be revealed in their flocks' hearts and lives.

71

Shepherding Implemented

Shepherding requires *accountability*. That is the only way to "keep watch" as Paul commanded. To have true accountability, you have to get real. If we hide behind our self-righteousness, we will never receive the help we need. Sharon Hersch says it well: "The greatest human creativity [music, art, and books] testifies to our human weakness. Yet our response to our personal brokenness is . . . to hide it, keep it at arm's length, numb it with addiction, cover it up with self-righteousness, and certainly not burden anyone else with it."[1] We knew that our members would not naturally disclose their brokenness and thus it would be hard to shepherd them. So what would we do?

We could have just assigned each elder to a certain number of people and told him to have a go, but we believed God had called us, and Scripture teaches us, to connect to our members in a relational way, at the heart level. To minister to someone at the heart level is not a drive-by event. It takes time and the movement of the Spirit. It includes regular, personal contact. It is too easy to care—or not to care—for someone by sending them a quick text or an email. Face-to-face and voice-to-voice are the ways of the Bible, and we knew we had to call elders to do that with people.

We started by assigning elders to people they knew, and we added new members to the assignments as they came. Over time we went after the people no one knew. We said to our elders, "The bottom line is that it is critical for you to identify who your sheep are, for them to know you are their shepherd, and for you to have regular and meaningful contact with them. If one of them

---

1. Sharon A. Hersh, *The Last Addiction: Own Your Desire, Live beyond Recovery, Find Lasting Freedom* (Colorado Springs: WaterBrook Press, 2008), 67.

is sick, we are counting on you to go to the hospital. If one of them dies, we are counting on you to assist with the funeral. We want you to know them well, and it is best if they live near you."

Once we had assigned elders to church members according to previous knowledge and by geography, we had to make sure they had tools and support. We did not want them to be underequipped or unmotivated for their work. We knew they needed accountability and a system to help them. Fortunately, many of the men were in the marketplace, and they were used to having databases and technological systems to support them in their work. Brandon Huff, our director of technology operations, worked with our church management system, MinistryPlatform, to develop a shepherding application that was custom-built for Perimeter Church.

At that point, we had developed the following shepherding strategy:

1. Every member household at Perimeter is connected to an elder. The ratio is roughly one elder for every seven households. The households live close to the elder.
2. Every elder is shepherded by a lead elder. Most lead elders shepherd six or seven elders and their families.
3. The congregation is divided by geography into four parishes. Each parish has an area pastor.
4. Our elders use the shepherding app designed by Brandon Huff and his team to check in on their member households. The phone app allows elders to view members' group activity, access members' addresses and other contact information, and see the names of everyone in a given family.
5. Elders are asked to contact their members regularly, preferably face-to-face or by phone. Text and email are not preferred.

6. After an elder makes contact, he puts a note in the shepherd-ing app.[2] The system is color-coded. If a note in the app is less than thirty days old, the member is marked green. If more than thirty days have passed since contact, the color changes to yellow. After sixty days without contact, the color changes to red.

7. Weekly reports are run by each parish to see how well we are doing overall. The area pastor encourages the elders in his parish to make contact with members who are yellow and red and to put a note in the app.[3]

8. Potential new officers are trained for their shepherding role. If they become elders, it is because they are gifted to shepherd people.

Implementing the shepherding structure requires dedication. Pastoral staff have to model shepherding to the elders. When I, as a pastor, call my lead elders and get to know them and serve them, they in turn call and get to know their elders, who in turn call and get to know their member households. And yes, there are seasons when all of us get behind with making calls, meet-ing members, and putting notes in the app. At those times, we remind men of the importance of making contact so that we can shepherd the flock of God that he bought with his blood.

As we implemented our shepherding structure, we gave our elders numerous in-service workshops about both the shepherding

---

2. Although the system is closed, elders are instructed to make notes generic: "I called the Smith family, and they asked me to pray for them about a situation" rather than "I called the Smith family, and they asked me to pray for their son, who is going through a sex-change operation."

3. Often it turns out that the elder has made contact but has not put a note in the system. There is a learning curve. All Perimeter elders have hearts to shepherd, but some are not as good with the technical aspect.

app and the care call in which they make contact with members.[4] We roleplayed. We created videos. We went over and over the training to help our elders to own the importance of the shepherding ministry.

Technology and Shepherding

Not every church needs a full-blown church management system (ChMS), but churches should *consider* using one.[5] Your church probably already has some type of basic system that could be configured to assist in its shepherding process. If you have a database system, ask your vendor about options for facilitating your church's shepherding process.

Of course, technology is a help, not the answer. Brandon Huff notes, "When I talk to churches, they generally get fixed on what system they should use and feel they can't move forward with shepherding without a technological system." But shepherding is about people connecting with people. Failure to settle on a ChMS should not be an excuse for failure to care for the flock.

Feeding God's sheep, tending his lambs, and guarding his flock is work. It is work worthy of the calling of an elder, and we praise God for the technology that makes it easier to know that we are fulfilling the call. From time to time, we hear from a member who is thrilled that they "have an elder" and that he

---

4. I have provided a script for care calls at the end of this chapter.

5. There are many ChMS on the market for well under one thousand dollars a year, and networking with other churches will give a church an idea of the limitations of each system. Some ChMS to consider include Shelby, ACS, Planning Center, Church Community Builder, Breeze (for smaller churches), and MinistryPlatform and Rock (for larger churches). This is not an exhaustive list. An even less expensive option would be a shareable spreadsheet program.

called them, connected with them, and prayed for them. In this high-tech, low-touch world, people want to know that they have been seen, that they have been noticed, that someone cares. It is our role to see them, listen to them, grieve with them, and then remind them of the love of Christ as we equip them for works of service to him.

Supplement: Sample Care Call Script

Here is a sample script for an elder care call:

Hi, my name is Randy Schlichting. I am an elder at your church, Perimeter Church, and I wonder if you have a few minutes to speak with me? (I promise you are not in trouble!) Thanks!

I am calling because we want to begin reaching out to people who live near us and see how they are doing. I think you live in _____, and that is where I live too. The main reason for my call is to see how I can pray for you, maybe help you to get connected or reconnected, and just see how you are doing. [Pause]

First, I want to say that I am glad you are a member of Perimeter. It means a lot to us as leaders that you come and participate with us. I have been at Perimeter for _____ years, and I have seen a lot of things change during that time. I have also been challenged in my spiritual growth and, like anyone else, I have had my ups and downs. As I said, I live in the same city that you live in, _____, so we may know some of the same people.

Anyway, I would love to get together with you and get to know you more. I would love to hear from you and hope to see you soon.

USER GUIDE

CREATING A CHURCH MANAGEMENT SYSTEM

DR. SCHLICHTING WRITES, "Not every church needs a full-blown church management system (ChMS), but churches should *consider* using one. Your church probably already has some type of basic system that could be configured to assist in its shepherding process. If you have a database system, ask your vendor about options for facilitating your church's shepherding process."

1. Discuss your church management system and consider how it might be useful in your shepherding ministry.
2. If you don't have a church management system, consider how you might use a simple spreadsheet or Google Docs.
3. What challenges might you encounter in setting up a computer- or phone-based system to record contacts with members? What would make those challenges worth it?
4. Contact a church that you know is working with technology to care for their people and see what you can learn.

For Further Reflection

1. Do your leaders know the spiritual condition of the members of your church? Why or why not?
2. How would you motivate elders to connect with households? How would you train them to make a care call?

6

Shepherding through Small Groups

Bijan Mirtolooi

IT WAS A Wednesday night in Lower Manhattan. A small group from Redeemer Presbyterian Church had gathered in a local restaurant to share a meal. In the group were men and women of different races, income levels, educational backgrounds, and political ideologies. The members of the group looked different, talked differently, and thought very differently about many important subjects. What they had in common, though, was that they were loved by Jesus Christ.

As they ate together, a woman from a nearby table walked over to them and said, "I'm sorry to interrupt your meal, but I have to ask: how is it that you all know each other?" As she had watched the group eat and talk and laugh together, she had wondered how these people who were so obviously different had formed such a strong bond. From that table emanated a sense of belonging, a sense of family.

A deep sense of community—of unity amid diversity—was a feature of the first Christian church, and because it reflects the heart of Jesus's prayer for his people before his death (John 17:21), it remains an ideal for the church today. Many churches realize this ideal by providing small groups for their members and regular attendees to share life together as a community.

Typically, small groups have trained lay leaders—ideally, two or more per group—who oversee and facilitate the group, and the system itself is overseen by the church's pastoral staff and elected leaders. Small groups meet consistently (weekly or biweekly), taking occasional breaks as needed throughout the year. Their size varies from five to fifteen people. Groups most often meet in people's homes, though third places such as coffee shops, community centers, or church buildings are also good options. As groups meet, they deepen friendships, pray with and for one another, read and study the Bible, provide accountability, and support one another, especially when one of their members is experiencing challenges.

Although many churches pursue small groups as a way of fostering community, small groups can also be an indispensable mechanism for providing pastoral care to every member of the church. The twofold purpose of this chapter is to describe *how* and *why* small groups can and should be part of a church's shepherding plan.

Notice that I said *part* of a church's shepherding plan. An ideal plan ought to situate a small-group system alongside Sunday worship and other mechanisms for direct elder or pastor contact for pastoral care. Small groups cannot and should not replace the gathered worship of the people of God, nor can they provide the precision and depth of care that is possible though pastoral visitation. This chapter presents shepherding through small groups as complementary with pastoral visitation and Sunday worship.

Why Shepherd through Small Groups?

The apostle Paul instructed the Ephesian elders, "Keep watch over . . . all the flock of which the Holy Spirit has made you overseers" (Acts 20:28 NIV). The goal of shepherding is discipleship: helping Christians to follow Jesus in every area of their lives. As pastors and elders discern how to provide care that disciples their church members, they must confront both practical and spiritual challenges.

The Challenge of Shepherding Comprehensively

The pastors and elders of any local church are responsible to shepherd every member of their congregation.[1] In this responsibility, a significant challenge is one of comprehensiveness. Pastors and elders must ask themselves, "Are we shepherding *all* the flock?"

I have served as an associate pastor of a large church, and I now serve as lead pastor for a smaller church. Whether a church is large or small, the challenge of comprehensiveness impacts how pastoral care is provided. Large churches have lots of members, but they also have bigger and more specialized staff teams. Smaller churches have fewer members to care for but also smaller staff and leadership teams to provide that care. No matter the size of a church, however, a small-group system can be used to ensure that every member of the congregation is cared for.

The Challenge of Nurturing Commitment

It is now all but taken for granted that Western culture is excessively individualistic. As people focus on themselves,

---

1. Throughout this chapter, *shepherd* and *provide pastoral care* are used interchangeably.

they become increasingly afraid of commitment. They fear to commit to something good because something better might eventually come along.[2] Small groups within the church foster a countercultural practice of commitment.[3] As part of a small group, members begin building relationships with others in their church family. Because a person does not handpick who is in their small group, group members often share life with people they would otherwise have nothing to do with. The small group becomes a band of unlikely friends who walk through life together.

Commitment to community is sometimes hard. Community can be messy. But through small groups Christians learn the countercultural practice of commitment even when it is uncomfortable and inconvenient. In small groups they learn how to be a family together and unlearn the habits of unhealthy individualism.

The Challenge of Fighting Spiritual Apathy

There was a time when members of churches wanted, even expected, their pastors to visit them. In the early 1980s, Thomas Oden described how church members would sometimes become angry if the pastor didn't call on them![4] How different things are today. Especially in larger churches, members often do not expect a pastor to reach out to them, and even when a pastor

2. See Mark Dever, *Nine Marks of a Healthy Church* (Wheaton, IL: Crossway, 2004), 147.

3. Pete Davis explores the unique beauty of a "Counterculture of Commitment . . . [the] radical act of making commitments to particular things—to particular places and communities, to particular causes and crafts, and to particular institutions and people" in *Dedicated: The Case for Commitment in an Age of Infinite Browsing* (New York: Avid Reader, 2021), 7.

4. See Thomas C. Oden, *Pastoral Theology: Essentials of Ministry* (San Francisco: Harper San Francisco, 1983), 169.

does, some respond ambivalently. Jen Pollock Michel describes the root of the problem this way: "One of the most seductive promises of a technological age [is] that ours should be an *unbothered* life. As our lives get easier, we are increasingly formed by the desire for ease. . . . This promise of unencumbered living is perhaps the most insidious danger and also the one we talk the least about."[5] In a time when spiritual apathy has seeped into churches, part of pastoral care means helping Christians to move from being passive consumers to active participants in the life of the church.

Sunday worship and even pastoral visitation, indispensable though they are, can be passive experiences for the average congregant. But every member of a small group eventually becomes an active participant in its life and ministry. As members of the group share insights from Scripture with one another, they realize that God can use their words to build others up. When members pray for one another, they assume a distinctly priestly function, carrying others to God as they bear them on their hearts (Ex. 28:29–30). When members of the group make a meal for another member in need, they act in a small but real way as the hands and feet of Jesus. To borrow language from Ed Welch, in small groups every Christian discovers that they are not only *needy* but also *needed*.[6] They begin to move away from holding the dangerous expectation of "unencumbered living" that Michel describes.

---

5. Jen Pollock Michel, "Move Over, Sex and Drugs. Ease is the New Vice," *Christianity Today,* January 31, 2019, https://www.christianitytoday.com/ct/2019/january-web-only/technology-move-over-sex-drugs-ease-is-new-vice.html.

6. Edward T. Welch, *Side by Side: Walking with Others in Wisdom and Love* (Wheaton, IL: Crossway, 2015), 11.

How to Shepherd through Small Groups

It is beyond the scope of this chapter to cover all the elements that go into making a healthy small group. The focus here is narrower: we will examine what needs to be true of a church's small-group system in order for it to provide effective shepherding.

An Effective Small-Group System Starts with Membership

A foundational conviction of this book is that the pastors and elders of a congregation are responsible for shepherding every *member* of their church. Although different churches and denominations have different ways for a person to become a member, *that* a church has a membership process is essential for pastoral care. It is through membership that a person commits to love and serve the church and the church commits to love and care for that person. Having a clear membership process is important, especially in larger and urban churches that are highly transient. As pastors and elders seek to determine whom they are responsible to shepherd, membership is the mechanism best suited to define that shepherding relationship.

When small groups are a church's main mechanism for pastoral care, the small-group system passes the comprehensiveness test only if the expectation is clearly set that being a member of the church means being a part of a small group. The church's membership class(es) must emphasize the importance of small groups in the life of the church. Pastors and elders must ensure that all prospective members of the church are connected to a small group when they meet for their membership interview.

Since many regular attendees visit or join a small group before they become members of a church, many people are already participating in small groups when they meet with a pastor or elder to pursue church membership. But for those who are not yet in small groups, the membership interview is a place for the pastor or elder to help them to get connected with small groups that fit their schedules and location needs.

An Effective Small-Group System Continues with Leadership

For a church to effectively shepherd members through a small-group system, much depends on the lay leaders of the small groups. The pastoral staff identifies, trains, and supports the lay leaders of the small groups, and those leaders care for the participants in their groups.

Identifying. The most straightforward approach to identifying new small-group leaders is to have existing leaders look at the participants of their small groups and prayerfully discern who among them has leadership potential. The next step is to entrust that prospective leader with responsibilities in the group, such as leading a prayer time or planning a social. If leadership gifts are affirmed, the prospective leader is invited into training.

Training.[7] When a small-group system serves as part of the church's shepherding plan, the lay leaders of the small groups are

---

7. New leaders can be trained to lead their small groups in myriad ways, and each such training needs to be, at some level, church specific so that it can account for the unique features of a local church. That said, if anyone is starting from scratch and wondering how to train their small-group leaders, a good place to begin is Timothy J. Keller, Jeffrey O. White, and Andrew E. Field, *Fellowship Group Handbook: A Manual for Leaders and Coordinators*, ver. 2.1 (New York: Redeemer Presbyterian Church, 1999). It is available for purchase online at https://gospelinlife.com/downloads /fellowship-group-handbook-pdf-format/.

pastoral care providers. Small-group leaders are not just hosts, discussion facilitators, or social organizers; they are under-shepherds in the congregation. Therefore, the training of new leaders for small groups must include helping them to carry out the four shepherding functions: knowing, feeding, leading, and protecting the members of their small group.[8]

The pastoral staff team at Redeemer Presbyterian Church West Side put together the following guide for training leaders of their small groups (now called *community groups* or *CGs*) in these four functions:

- *Know*: leader knows their members well
  - Keep CG member roster up to date
  - Know the general spiritual health of members
  - Routinely ask about life updates in person, at CG meetings, or over email/phone
  - Know if and where CG members worship and if they are worshipping regularly
  - Know the current prayer requests of CG members
  - Celebrate and weep with members (Rom. 12:15)
- *Feed*: leader helps to give their members the means of grace
  - Facilitate Bible discussion during CG meetings
  - Take advantage of Bible teaching classes offered by the church
  - Model personal and cultural winsomeness when handling the Bible and Christian teachings
- *Lead*: leader leads their group life and models spiritual leadership
  - Organize or delegate service projects every 1–3 months

---

8. See Timothy Z. Witmer, *The Shepherd Leader: Achieving Effective Shepherding in Your Church* (Phillipsburg, NJ: P&R Publishing, 2010), chapters 5–8.

- ○ Delegate aspects of CG meetings and life together (e.g., socials) to members and future leaders
- ○ Help members to participate in ongoing personal discipleship practices
- *Protect*: leader helps to protect members from spiritual harm
  - ○ Know when and how to triage difficult relational and spiritual cases of members
  - ○ Ensure CG is a safe and confidential place for members
  - ○ Understand the basics of the Christian faith, and the church's teaching, so they are able to answer questions and represent the church as questions arise[9]

Supporting. If you're wondering whether providing pastoral care for their small groups is too much of a burden for lay leaders to carry, this is where the pastoral staff and elders of the church fit in. In addition to training lay leaders to carry out their tasks, they also need to support them.[10] The care that they provide is twofold: they encourage the leaders in their own walk with Christ and support them in their leadership role. They should aim to connect with their small-group leaders at least once per month. Those connections may happen in person, over a phone call or Zoom, or as a brief catch-up before or after a Sunday worship service. The way pastoral staff and elders care for the leaders to

9. Unpublished community group leaders' training material, created by the community group staff team of Redeemer Presbyterian Church West Side in 2018.

10. Pastoral staff share a fundamental identity with elders who are not full-time staff members: they are shepherds. What differs between them is the scope to which they carry out the work of shepherding. Pastoral staff can devote most of their working weeks to caring for the flock, while elders necessarily have less time to do so. In my experience, a person on the church's pastoral staff can effectively oversee twenty to thirty small groups and their leaders, while an elder can effectively oversee three to five.

which they are assigned matters—small group leaders show care in the same way they receive care.

To assign pastoral staff and elders to groups, some churches use a parish or neighborhood-based model, while others employ a different approach. However the assignments are made, what is vital is that the relationship be clear. Every small-group leader should know which pastoral staff member or elder supports them, and every pastoral staff member and elder should know which groups and leaders they oversee.

It may be helpful to envision a church's small-group system as a pyramid with the pastoral staff and elders at the top. The pastoral staff and elders provide direct care for the lay leaders of the small groups. The lay leaders in turn provide direct care for the members of their small groups with the support and guidance of the pastoral staff member or elder who is overseeing them. As a pastoral staff member or an elder cares for a lay leader, they are available to coach the leader when crises or acute challenges emerge in the leader's small group. If the lay leader is not qualified or able to provide care in a particular situation, they can quickly and smoothly triage the need to the pastoral staff or elder who is assigned to them.

In this system, every member of the church is under the shepherding care of the pastoral team or elders—sometimes indirectly, as in the case of the small-group members, and sometimes directly, as in the case of the small-group leaders. Consider one example, representative of many, of how this plays out. A man in his early thirties was diagnosed with an aggressive form of lymphoma. He quickly let his small group know, and the wheels of care began to turn. The other members of the group helped with practical needs such as chores and meals for his family. The leaders of the small group listened to and prayed with the man as he asked honest questions about God's purposes in his suffering.

And the lay leaders kept the elder who oversaw the group aware of the situation, which enabled a few pastors and elders to visit the young man in the hospital for healing prayer. In this way, a small-group system is uniquely able to provide comprehensive care for members of a church by offering shepherding from both lay leaders and elders.

An Effective Small-Group System Depends on Updated Rosters

Updating rosters may not be the most exhilarating part of pastoral care! But keeping rosters accurate and up-to-date is essential. For the small-group system to continue to pass the comprehensiveness test, rosters must correctly indicate which church members are part of which small group.

There is no shortage of online platforms that churches can use to post sign-ups and rosters for small groups. Some churches, especially larger ones, choose to build their own platforms, which they can integrate with other systems they are using.[11] The pastoral staff, the elders, or even the church's support staff should provide biannual or quarterly reminders for all small-group leaders to update their rosters. This ensures that participation within small groups will be tracked accurately.

A Word of Caution

Soon or later, every shepherding program faces the test of comprehensiveness. If not every sheep is accounted for, the

---

11. See chapter 5, "*Knowing* Every Member (with a Technological Assist)," for more guidance in this area.

shepherding plan is not comprehensive.[12] Thus, in employing a small-group system as a shepherding plan, one of two directions must be taken. Either (1) the small-group system must sit alongside another system of elder contact, and both must work together to provide comprehensive care, or (2) great attention must be given to ensure that the small-group system itself accounts for every member. As someone who believes deeply in the importance of small-group systems for effective shepherding, even I have seen and experienced how easy it is for them to fail the comprehensive test.

But no one said shepherding the flock of God would be easy. For all the times and in the all the ways that pastors and elders have failed to care for all the flock, there is grace in Christ, the Chief Shepherd (1 Peter 5:4). When they are renewed in grace and relying on the Spirit, pastors and elders can give themselves over to the good work of caring for all the flock, which the Lord Jesus bought with his own blood (Acts 20:28). The words of J. I. Packer could not be more apt: once a leader is convinced that his calling is to shepherd the whole flock, "it will not be beyond us to find a method of doing it that suits our situation; where there's a will, there's a way!"[13]

---

12. See Witmer, *Shepherd Leader*, 198, 206.

13. J. I. Packer, introduction to *The Reformed Pastor* by Richard Baxter (repr., Edinburgh: Banner of Truth, 1979), 19.

USER GUIDE

THE USE OF SMALL GROUPS IN YOUR CHURCH

CHAPTER 6 CITED individualism and apathy as challenges to discipleship. What other discipleship challenges exist in your ministry context that a small group system might help to confront?

If your church has a small-group system in place already, take a moment to evaluate it. How is that system doing as a mechanism for shepherding every member of your church? What are some areas in which it needs to grow?

If your church does not have a small-group system in place already, consider how one might enhance your ability to provide comprehensive and proactive care for every member of your church.

How are lay leaders developed and supported in your church? Reflect on how a small-group system could enhance your pipeline for lay leader formation and development.

Ed Welch writes that every Christian is both needy and needed. In what way do small groups function as prime contexts for every Christian to live out that truth? Reflect for a few moments on how the gospel creates a unique kind of human community that enables people to see themselves both as being needy of others and as those who have something to contribute to strengthening their church and community.

For Further Reflection

1. If you shepherd your members through small groups, is every member of your church in a small group? If not, what might you do about this?
2. If your strategy is to shepherd through small groups, do your members understand that strategy? How have you communicated it to them, and how might you improve this communication?
3. If your small-group leaders are not officers in your church, what mechanism do you have in place so they can communicate with elders?

7

WOMEN CARING FOR WOMEN IN SUPPORT OF YOUR SHEPHERDING MINISTRY

SUE HARRIS

YEARS AGO, I was a Bible study teacher and seminary student. I loved ministering to the women of our church, but, although I was viewed as a leader of women, I had no real title or responsibility.

One evening, while attending a women's ministry event sponsored by my church, I found myself sitting near a young wife and mother whom I'd known for a few years. That night she was acting strange. Her humor had always been slightly edgy, which usually made for a lot of fun, but on this particular evening she crossed a line. Actually, she crossed a number of lines as her jokes went from irreverent to crass. When I gently challenged her, she seemed to move on.

Later, I was bothered in my spirit but wasn't sure what I ought to do next. I pursued her the next Sunday in church and asked if we could talk privately. I had read Paul Tripp's book *Instruments in the Redeemer's Hands* and was aware that root sins often lie behind fruit sins.[1] There was something deeper driving her irreverent humor and inappropriate joking, and I asked what it was.

As if she'd been waiting for the dam to break, the woman buried her head in her hands and began to cry. She revealed that her marriage was in shambles. She told me that her husband was sexually, physically, and emotionally abusive. She told me that no one knew what was happening in her home—only me—and said she couldn't carry the burden alone any longer.

After our long and exhausting conversation, I knew I was out of my depth. Was this true? I couldn't understand how a man I'd known for years could be guilty of such things, and I was slightly concerned he would be waiting for me in the empty church parking lot as I left the building. I walked to my car stunned and overwhelmed. What was my next step? What would we as a church do to help?

From my car, I reached out to an elder and my pastor. Although equally surprised, they quickly put together a plan to protect the woman and to interview her husband. But, by the end of the next day, less than twenty-four hours after her confession to me, the woman recanted her entire story and claimed I had fabricated it. Furthermore, her husband accused me of lying and called me at my workplace, threatening me. He lectured me about submission and told me my word would never have any authority over his. It seemed like he was trying to intimidate me into leaving the church. Soon after, the family resigned their membership at our church and quickly joined another.

I was saddened by the whole situation. A woman who needed protection and healing had never received it. My brothers and

---

1. Paul David Tripp, *Instruments in the Redeemer's Hands: People in Need of Change Helping People in Need of Change* (Phillipsburg, NJ: P&R Publishing, 2002), 60.

elders in the church wanted to do more, but we were all perplexed. I knew we, as a body of believers, could do better. We needed a structure that could better care for the vulnerable, and we needed to use wisdom from both men and women to shepherd the flock. But how?

Problem and Solution

Churches often find it difficult to establish a shepherding system that submits to sound doctrine while including women. Churches may desire to shepherd their entire flocks, but many that are committed to male ordination focus on equipping and using only ordained males. This can create a gap in shepherding and care.

The solution is for church leadership to commission women to proactively and protectively shepherd other women in the church, alongside the shepherding elders. At Oak Mountain Presbyterian Church (OMPC), a shepherding team of one hundred forty (which includes fifty-seven female members) share the honor and burden of caring for a 2,800-member congregation. Women are selected, examined, trained, and commissioned annually. They stand shoulder to shoulder with their brothers as they help to ensure that the entire congregation is shepherded.

Why Shepherding Women?

Women likely make up at least half of the adults in your pews. Readily available statistics indicate that many of these women will experience infertility or miscarriages in the course of their lives, and many more have experienced, or will experience, sexual harassment, assault, rape, or other forms of violence—even at the hands of their husbands or boyfriends. Many may be struggling with depression, which is more prevalent in women than in men.[2] It is likely that some in your congregation have gotten abortions or know others who have, and it is almost certain that some are viewing porn on a regular basis. These are the women in your pews.

When OMPC commissions new women to serve as shepherds, they complete an assessment that includes a theological examination and asks for a testimony to the gospel of grace in their lives. Without exception, every year we hear testimonies that represent the common struggles of women in the pews. We know that believers often minister most deeply out of their own sufferings (2 Cor. 1:3–4). The women who join the men in shepherding are sinners and sufferers along with those whom the elders desire to shepherd. They understand the landscape of living life as women—this knowledge is naturally available to them in a way it is not for men. This is not to say that ministry is ever easy or even second nature to anyone, but women want to help their brothers to minister to the full body of Christ. Look again at the previous paragraph and know that some women in your church are asking, "Would you like help with this?"

When we began to develop our shepherding model at OMPC, our shepherd elders quickly realized they didn't want to do the job alone. It wasn't that they *couldn't* do the job—they simply recognized that they could shepherd more effectively with the help of trusted, faithful, orthodox, examined, and trained women. They requested their help.

Dan Doriani writes,

2. "Depression in Women: Understanding the Gender Gap," Mayo Clinic, January 29, 2019, https://www.mayoclinic.org/diseases-conditions/depression/in-depth/depression/art-20047725.

When a group [church] exceeds the size of 150, it becomes impossible for everyone to know everyone. Then elders need trusted eyes and ears, especially to care for women and children. Married men do not easily oversee single and divorced women. Because mature women naturally and properly retain closer contact with them, they can help oversee them.

Someone may say, "Elders can gain this information by talking to their wives." True, but not all elders are married. (Since Jesus was single, we must either permit single men to be elders or set standards that Jesus did not meet.) Further, wise women may not be married to elders or may not be married at all. Besides, elders do not always consult their wives as well as they could. Above all, by consulting wise women, leaders can act on the point that women like Deborah, Abigail, and Priscilla dispensed excellent and timely counsel.[3]

Excellent and timely counsel is what we're all looking for, isn't it? As your church develops a shepherding system, find your present-day Deborahs, Abigails, and Priscillas. They are likely already steady worshippers in your church. They bring value to your congregation and will bring wisdom to shepherding relationships as they stand shoulder to shoulder with the shepherding elders.

Doriani anticipates concerns and questions regarding the limitations on leadership roles for women and writes,

Men will have questions. Should pastors then consult women about their preaching? Why not—at least to learn more about the church's needs? Will women gain too much authority if men consult them so? This alleged problem was not on Josiah's mind

3. Dan Doriani, *Women and Ministry: What the Bible Teaches* (Wheaton, IL: Crossway, 2003), 129.

when he consulted Huldah or on David's mind when Abigail talked sense into him! Will the presence of women disrupt the atmosphere of meetings formerly run by men alone? Maybe, but some all-male men's meetings could use a little disruption. . . . Women's relational sensibility can balance the goals-and-management perspectives of men.[4]

The truth is that most churches already have women in their congregations who are pouring into others. Our goal is to make sure those women receive theological training and are equipped for ministry, then integrated into a lay pastoral care structure so that others can draw on their wisdom in an organized, intentional, and regulated way. Women are not the secret weapon of shepherding, nor are they better than men, nor do they have all the answers that are somehow hidden from men. Women do, however, provide insight that might escape men and help to alleviate their burden as they shepherd women. It is wonderful to see men and women partner to care for the full body of believers in a church.

Selection, Training, and Commissioning

If you're convinced that you should equip women to help with the shepherding in your church, how should you proceed?

Selection

The first step is to find the women in your church who have shepherds' hearts and routinely act as shepherd leaders within

4. Doriani, 129–30.

your church family. Often this can be done by leaders who are in a position to observe unofficial shepherding, such as a women's ministry director. At OMPC, we can receive names for consideration from any leader within the church; however, normally the shepherding pastor, adult discipleship pastor, and women's ministry director are the ones who recruit members. You may wish to identify a specific leader or leaders who can assemble a shepherding checklist that is consistent with your shepherding process and can then approve potential recruits.

At OMPC, women are vetted by the shepherding pastor, adult discipleship pastor, and women's ministry director. If they meet with unanimous approval, their names are submitted to the senior pastor for his approval as well.

Vetting

A woman may be disqualified for service even if she has a shepherd's heart. At OMPC, we ask the following questions to assess a potential recruit.

- *How long has she been a member of the church?* We require someone to be a member of OMPC for at least two years before we consider her for this role. This gives us time to get to know her.
- *Does she attend church services?* At OMPC, anyone who attends worship less than half the time is disqualified from a shepherding role. Regular church attendance evidences faithful service, submission to the leaders of the church, and a mature ecclesiology. Practically speaking, shepherding often happens on Sunday mornings in the pews. We value church attendance and want to work with women who do the same.

- *Does she have enormous personal or family struggles and obligations?* These could disqualify someone from shepherding for a season.
- *Is she a team player?* A shepherd's primary function is to ensure that the flock is being cared for and to work with her brothers and sisters in that endeavor. A woman may be disqualified if she has a tendency to create disunity.
- *Is she given to gossip?* Nothing cuts off a shepherding ministry's head quicker than gossip. If the women in your church can't trust those who serve as shepherds, their ministry will be debilitated.
- *Does she have theological views or other personal agendas that appear to conflict with the mission of shepherding care?* Anyone who undermines the shepherding ministry or structure is disqualified for service.

Training

Once women have been recruited, they must be trained. The nature of this training depends on what is important to your church's leadership and the development of its shepherding structure. Since OMPC is part of the Presbyterian Church in America, we spend significant time teaching Reformed and Presbyterian distinctives and examining the women's understanding of these. We train them in both doctrine and practical theology using the Westminster Confession of Faith, Louis Berkhof's *Summary of Christian Doctrine*, and Paul Tripp's *Instruments in the Redeemer's Hands*.

At the end of eight weeks of training, each candidate completes a written assessment of her orthodoxy, practical theology, and spiritual maturity. We also ask her testimonial questions so we can ascertain her ability to communicate her personal story with clarity and orthodoxy. After passing this examination, women are approved by our session and commissioned for service.

Commissioning

Finally, OMPC *publicly* commissions its new shepherding women. This is an essential part of their role. It establishes that the shepherding team is not one to be joined simply by raising one's hand. During a worship service, our senior pastor defines the shepherding role these women will fill, differentiating their commission from ordination and explaining our recruiting, training, and examining process. The women take vows, and our shepherding elders commission them for service.

The annual commissioning service is a gift to the congregation as well as to the commissioned women. It provides the entire church with an opportunity to see women in leadership, recognize their value to the elders of the church, and learn about their contribution to the shepherding process.

Men and Women Working Together to Shepherd

Women provide a different kind of care from men and a different set of gifts. God made men and women to work together. He created Eve as a "necessary ally" for Adam.[5] He created both men and women in his image (Gen. 1:27), and the dominion mandate falls to both (Gen. 1:26). Paul reminds Timothy that the church is a household (1 Tim. 3:15) and that we interact with one

---

5. John McKinley, "Necessary Allies: God as Ezer, Woman as Ezer," lecture, Hilton Atlanta, November 17, 2015, mp3 download, 38:35, http://www.wordmp3 .com/details.aspx?id=20759. Quoted in Aimee Byrd, *No Little Women: Equipping All Women in the Household of God* (Phillipsburg, NJ: P&R Publishing, 2016), 25.

another as fathers, brothers, mothers, and sisters (1 Tim. 5:1–2). The church ought to lead the world in the way we normalize this sort of teamwork. The family of God, both brothers and sisters, ought to live out what it looks like to care deeply for one another.[6]

Often churches, however, will avoid mixed groups and discourage friendships and ministry partnerships with men and women who are not married to one another. But we believe their blessing far outweighs their risk. As men and women work together to shepherd hurting people, their combined wisdom and insight can bring healing in a special way. For example, the presence of women in a shepherding team can lead both men and women to respond to the team with more vulnerability as they open themselves up for help.[7]

It does, however, take discipline and significant effort to put together an integrated shepherding structure in which men and women work together. Any women's ministry director or coordinator can put together a care team for women, but integrated proactive shepherding is more than that. The shepherding women's team is embedded in the shepherding elders' team at OMPC and follows the structure of commitment, encouragement, accountability, and equipping, especially for crisis. Shepherding elders and shepherding women attend monthly leadership meetings to receive ongoing training and equipping for improved shepherding. These mixed-sex groups pray together, encourage one another, and labor side by side to build up the body of Christ. They discuss general congregational trends as well as specific ways they can pursue the men and women assigned to them.[8]

6. See Thompson, *Soul of Desire*, 111.

7. See Curt Thompson, *The Soul of Desire: Discovering the Neuroscience of Longing, Beauty, and Community* (Downers Grove, IL: IVP, 2021), 109.

8. Ken Jones discusses this in more detail in chapter 2, "Four Principles for an Effective Shepherding Structure."

Every household at OMPC has a shepherding elder. If an adult woman lives in that household, she also has a shepherding woman assigned to her. This is not to say that OMPC has taken the responsibility of shepherding women away from our ordained shepherding elders. We encourage our elders to maintain godly contact with the women under their care. Some feel uncomfortable calling, texting, or even emailing women who are not their wives, sisters, or mothers, so we provide some guidelines and training on how to do this well,[9] and we remind our shepherding elders to draw on the wisdom of the shepherding women if they have concerns.

No, OMPC's shepherding elders are not excused from their responsibility to shepherd women just because we use a women's shepherding team. But our shepherding elders have an unbelievable and unquantifiable advantage in shepherding because they have the women's shepherding team to help them. These women come alongside them and stand shoulder to shoulder with them as they follow the Good Shepherd, who is our Savior, Rescuer, Provider, Protector, Pursuer, Bridegroom, and Elder Brother.

I often wonder what would have happened to the woman from the opening story if we had had the shepherding structure in place that we have today. If she'd had a trusted Christian brother—her shepherding elder— and a trained and commissioned shepherding woman to reach out to her, pursue her consistently, and pray for her . . . what would have been different? I'm not sure. But in my heart I think we would have had a better result.

---

9. A young elder at OMPC told me that as soon as he was given his list of men and women to shepherd, he immediately sent out the following text *to the women*: "Hello. My name is _____. I am your shepherding elder from OMPC. Please save my number in your phone. I'll be reaching out to you from time to time to check on you and find out how I can pray for you. You also have a woman shepherd. Her name is _____. You'll be hearing from her too. She's also committed to praying for and caring for you."

YOUR CHURCH'S MINISTRY TO WOMEN

WHEN MAKING SHEPHERDING contacts, elders often speak to the male head of a family. Other times, a wife answers and then passes the phone to her husband. It is certainly wise to speak to the head of a household, but what if the wife is bearing a burden she needs to share? Doesn't the lack of a strategy to shepherd the women of the church represent a failure of the comprehensive goal to shepherd *every* member?

Adding women to help with caring for the women of the church adds a blessed "redundancy" to the shepherding ministry.

- Pray for the wisdom to identify women who would serve well in this caring role. Provide training for the women who agree to serve.
- Be sure the members understand the motivation for this ministry.
- Be clear that these women are serving *in support* of the elders and are accountable to them.
- Begin your ministry to women in the church by reaching out to widows and single mothers.

For Further Reflection

1. How are you currently reaching out to and caring for the women of your church?
2. What would a women's shepherding team add to your congregation's shepherding ministry?
3. What do you think would be the best way to implement a women's shepherding team in your church?

PART 3

SHEPHERDING AND ADVANCING THE GOSPEL

8

EFFECTIVE SHEPHERDING IN A CHURCH-PLANTING CONTEXT

MARK HALLOCK

"IN A TIME when many church plants are permanently closing their doors, your congregation is thriving! The Lord is moving in power, and lives are being transformed throughout your congregation. What exactly are you and your leaders doing that is working so well?"

I was speaking to a church-planting friend of mine by the name of John. John's congregation has experienced healthy, steady growth over the five years since it was launched, but not for the reasons you would expect. His church was planted in a small town in the Midwest—not exactly an exploding metropolis. It wasn't planted with impressive financial resources or with a large group of gifted individuals to make up its core team. It wasn't heavily promoted by its denomination or by others in its community. And yet today this church is full of life and effectively reaching its community with the gospel in all kinds of biblically faithful, God-honoring ways.

I reached out to John with the hope of picking his brain on some of the key reasons for the health and growth his church had experienced. Was there something unique in their approach? What could other church planters learn from John and his team?

As I talked to John, it quickly became clear that he and his leaders shared something that sadly has become somewhat rare in the world of church planting: *a deep passion and a purposeful plan to shepherd God's people with intentional, Christlike care.* A passion and a plan. You see, John and his leaders have worked hard to develop a strategy that helps them to carry out effective biblical shepherding on a weekly basis. If you ask people in many church-planting circles about the key to starting, growing, and sustaining a healthy congregation, "intentional shepherding" is not typically the answer you hear. Yet I truly believe that what is happening in John's church can and should be true of new plants all across North America and the world.

The question is why we don't see an emphasis on passionate, purposeful shepherding as a core component of more church-planting philosophies in our day. Why is intentional shepherding often overlooked and neglected in light of other emphases in church multiplication?

To help to answer those questions, we must first identify and acknowledge some real challenges every church planter faces. Let's consider five of these.

Five Challenges to Effective Shepherding in a Church-Planting Context

Reaching New People While Shepherding Those Already in the Church

When planting a church, leaders must have the ongoing conviction and desire to reach their community and connect with those who don't know Jesus. This is a good thing. An important thing. I mean, this is one of the main reasons why new churches are planted in the first place, right? To take the gospel to people who desperately need Jesus. Of course, the challenge comes from trying to shepherd those who are already part of the congregation while at the same time reaching the lost outside it. It can be very difficult for a church planter and his leaders to balance these two priorities.

There are two ditches we want to avoid here. The first ditch is spending far more time than we should out in the community, neglecting the sheep who are already under our care. This creates frustration among the congregation and causes a pastor to quickly lose credibility and trust. The other ditch is spending far too much time with those inside the walls of the church plant, to the neglect of the lost in the community.[1] Falling into this ditch results in a failure to connect in a meaningful way with unbelievers and ultimately defeats the purpose for which the church was planted in the first place.

Both ditches are to be avoided at all costs. Those who are called to be church planters must have *both* a passion to reach those who are far from Christ and a deep love for faithfully shepherding God's people.

Meeting the Expectations of All Parties Involved

Another major challenge to shepherding as a church planter is the pressure from denominational leaders, partner churches, and individual supporters to grow a large church—and quickly. In one large denomination, a church planter is expected to meet and engage with a hundred new people in a hundred days. As you can

---

1. See chapter 9, "Shepherding and the Gospel Call," for more on this.

imagine, this takes a lot of time, energy, and commitment, leaving very little time for him to care well for the members already committed to the congregation. Sadly, many church planters feel the pressure to share stories with outside leaders and supporters about "all the new people" they are reaching with the gospel, but stories of faithful shepherding are often not valued in the same way. Feeling like you have to "sell" your church plant to get financial support is a heavy burden that many church planters constantly carry. It can suck the life and joy out of ministry.

Of course, the biggest problem with this is the assumption that large numbers of warm bodies are a sign of church health. While numerical growth *can* be a sign of health, it doesn't guarantee it. This is why many planters, as well as denominational leaders, need to adjust their understanding of what true, biblical success looks like in a church plant. Is the goal to get large numbers of people to show up on Sunday mornings, or is the goal the faithful shepherding care of the individual souls God entrusts to us, whatever their number may be?

Overcoming an Education Gap on Strategic Shepherding

Several years ago I spoke at a luncheon at a large evangelical seminary about the importance of biblical shepherding. After I spoke, a student came up to me and said something I will never forget. He said, "This is the first time in my three years at this seminary that anyone has spoken about the importance of shepherding God's people and what that might look like practically in the local church. In all the classes I have taken, there hasn't been one class focused on what you talked about today. Being a shepherd of God's people is what I feel called to be!"

At first, I thought this young man was joking. How could someone go through all the coursework for a master of divinity degree and not have a single class on pastoral shepherding in the local church? Sadly, he was dead serious. And the truth is I have met many seminarians over the past several years who have said similar things. There is a crisis in many of our seminaries when classes focused on business strategies, entrepreneurial skills, and the effective use of social media have taken the place of preparing future pastors to shepherd God's people with intentionality, love, grace, and truth. This is a real challenge. As a result, many young pastors, and specifically church planters, lack any kind of intentional shepherding vision and strategy when they head out to lead a church.

Avoiding Burnout in Core Team Members

One of the unique challenges that the large majority of church planters face is the ongoing need for volunteers to help set up and tear down for the worship gathering every Sunday morning. Along with this comes setting up for the children's ministry, making sure the worship team is prepared and the sound system is working, putting out signs in front of the meeting space so people can find where the church is gathering, ensuring that greeters are positioned to welcome people warmly, printing off and distributing the weekly bulletin or worship folder . . . I could go on and on. On a weekly basis, this can be a real grind—not only for the church planter but on all the faithful volunteers who are working together to pull this church off!

Unfortunately, church planters can get so focused on enlisting members to be volunteers that they forget these people too are individuals who need to be shepherded intentionally. You can imagine where this eventually leads. All too often, core team members and other volunteers get burned out serving a new church plant and lose the sense of joy they had at the beginning.

They can easily feel as though they are simply being used, not loved and cared for. Helping volunteers to feel appreciated, encouraged, and healthy is a shepherding challenge for every church planter.

Losing Members and Attendees

For most church planters, there's nothing more exciting than envisioning their new churches growing in healthy ways, over many years, making an eternal impact in their communities for the sake of the gospel. The thought of doing this with the same faithful group of Christian brothers and sisters, year in and year out, is a source of great joy. Unfortunately, it doesn't take long for many families and individuals, even those who seemed committed to the church plant for the long haul, to jump ship. Of course, they jump ship for a number of reasons, but, other than a physical move to another town, the reasons typically have one common denominator: *unmet expectations*. The church plant simply isn't all they thought it would be.

It's hard to describe just how painful it can be for planters when people they know and love are regularly leaving their churches, especially in the early years. This kind of transience makes it incredibly difficult for pastors to effectively shepherd a new congregation. Many church planters say the high turnover rate is their greatest challenge to creating a culture of shepherding care. When it is hard to pin down who is in and who is out, who is coming and who is going, strategic shepherding can feel next to impossible. It is hard to know whom to invest in and pour your life into when you don't know how long anyone will be around.

These are five real challenges when it comes to shepherding in a church-planting context. The question is, what do we do about them? If intentional shepherding is central to a healthy, biblical church plant, how do we counter these common challenges? What are some strategies we can implement to see biblical shepherding become not just a "good idea" but a lived-out reality?

Strategies for Effective Shepherding in a Church-Planting Context

Over the past ten years, the Lord has graciously allowed our church, Calvary Church in Englewood, Colorado, to become a multiplying congregation that has helped to plant or replant around thirty churches in the western United States. It has been an incredible joy to see lost people saved and disciples made in different communities as new churches are planted, and dying churches are replanted, for the glory of God. Over the course of these ten years, there are many things we have learned. We have made plenty of mistakes, that is for sure! But in his kindness, the Lord has allowed us to identify some important, timeless, biblical strategies that have been effective in each unique context where we have started a new church. *At the top of the list is the implementation of an intentional, comprehensive shepherding strategy.*

In our experience, such a shepherding strategy not only ensures the proper care of God's people but helps a church plant to grow in both numbers and spiritual health. Moreover, it fuels the multiplication of new church plants. Let me briefly share three reasons why this is the case.

First of all, church planting begins by making fully devoted disciples of Jesus in an established local church. When individual sheep are shepherded with deep love and sound biblical instruction, they grow and mature as disciples. As these growing and maturing disciples seek to obey Christ's Great Commission, they will grow faithful, shepherding congregations that will lead to the multiplication of new disciples through their ministry.

Second, when individuals are part of a church where they are shepherded well, they increasingly buy into the vision and mission of that congregation. As a result, a church that cares about both healthy, biblical shepherding and the multiplication of new congregations often raises up church-planting teams that are excited to transfer that same DNA to a new church plant.

Third, intentional shepherding helps pastors and leaders to know their people well. If churches are going to multiply, pastors must know how to best equip, encourage, and lead those who will eventually become the core group of a new congregation. Again, to lead people to live on mission in this way, pastors and leaders must have invested in intentional shepherding in order to know their people well. This is the foundation for a strong church plant.

At the end of the day, nothing is more important in church planting and church multiplication than effective shepherding. Nothing is more important than seeking to faithfully carry out the exhortation Paul gave to the Ephesian elders: "Be on guard for yourselves and for all the flock of which the Holy Spirit has appointed you as overseers, to shepherd the church of God, which he purchased with his own blood" (Acts 20:28 csb). Moreover, nothing closes the "back door" of a church plant like an intentional shepherding strategy. This isn't because shepherding is some kind of magic bullet. It is because Christlike, grace-filled, biblical shepherding is God's desire and design for the local church.

I said earlier that an effective shepherding strategy must be both intentional and comprehensive. It must be *intentional* in that it must be purposeful. It must have a clearly laid-out, strategic plan for what shepherding the flock will look like in a church-planting context *and* how it will be carried out. The strategy must be *comprehensive* in that it must include every person in the entire congregation, from the youngest to the oldest, from the nursery to the nursing home. True biblical shepherding is mindful of the entire flock and cares for it comprehensively.

So then, practically speaking, what are some specific strategies that can help us to carry out an intentional, comprehensive shepherding plan in a church plant? Let's consider several.

Make Shepherding a Top Priority from the Beginning

In the midst of so many different pressures and responsibilities, if a church planter does not make shepherding a top priority from the very beginning, it will easily fall to the wayside. It is much harder to create and implement an effective shepherding strategy sometime down the road. Often that day never comes. Shepherding must be prioritized from the very beginning.

Many church planters mistakenly assume the pastor and elders will "get serious" about shepherding once the congregation is bigger in number. The truth is, if intentional shepherding isn't a priority at the time of a church's initial launch, it most likely will never become one. Why? As a congregation increases in size, countless other programs, events, and leadership responsibilities drown out quality shepherding care. Again, implementing intentional shepherding strategies from the very beginning, even when the congregation is just a handful of people, is critical. The fruit that comes in time from making a shepherding commitment a top priority is incalculable.

Form a Shepherding Team and Meet Together Regularly

Many church planters aren't blessed to start out with a strong team of pastors and elders to help them shepherd the flock, as wonderful as that would be! For this reason, it doesn't take long for them to feel overwhelmed by all the shepherding needs that arise. What is a church planter to do? His hope and prayer is that additional pastors and elders will be raised up over time. However, this doesn't mean he can't immediately form a shepherding team to assist him in caring for the needs of the congregation.

What exactly do I mean by a *shepherding team*? I am speaking here of a team of trusted, mature, faithful men and women[2] who desire to help the church-planting pastor to care for and shepherd the flock. For example, you might invite small-group leaders, Sunday School teachers, or other key volunteers to be part of a shepherding team. These folks may not be elders or deacons, but they love God, love people, and desire to help the pastor to care for the congregation. This kind of team can be immensely helpful in creating a shepherding culture in a church plant.

I would encourage this group to meet once or twice a month. A shepherding team meeting should have six primary goals:

1. Celebrate the work God is doing in the lives of people, young and old, in the church plant. Spend a few minutes sharing stories and praising God for his work!
2. Look over the attendance sheets from the past month (see the next section), making note of any trends.
3. Discuss the specific shepherding needs of individuals in the congregation. Any upcoming surgeries? Any babies on the way? Is anyone in need of meals or a home visit? Which needs can be addressed by those on the shepherding team or by others in the congregation, and which should be addressed directly by the pastor?

2. These women can minister specifically to other women in the church plant. See chapter 7, "Women Caring for Women in Support of Your Shepherding Ministry."

4. Update the contact information for both regular attenders and visitors.
5. Share the names of visitors and guests and discuss a plan for the pastor and others on the shepherding team to follow up with them.
6. Pray for the congregation as a whole and for specific individuals.

When the church planter regularly meets with others who are helping to carry the shepherding load, he will be greatly encouraged in his work.

Make the Most of Sunday Worship Gatherings

The Sunday morning worship gathering is a prime time for God's people to connect with and care for one another. A church planter would be wise to make the most of this window of time each week. Let me propose three important shepherding goals for Sunday mornings.

Check in with church members and regular attenders. It is difficult for one pastor to spend time with every person who shows up on a Sunday morning. But if you have a team approach, others can relay information and prayer requests to the pastor so he can follow up with individuals throughout the week. For this reason, Sunday mornings are a prime time to have your shepherding team in place, ready, and mobilized to check in with members and regular attenders. I would recommend creating a system for recording shepherding needs, prayer requests, and personal updates so that they can be passed on to the pastor and other relevant parties.

Take attendance weekly. Keeping track of people's worship attendance and program or ministry involvement is crucial to creating a shepherding culture in which they are known, fed, led, and protected. The attendance that is taken should include every child, teenager, and adult each Sunday. Taking attendance helps the pastor and other leaders to know who's visiting, who's on the fringe, who's in, and who's out.

Although there are different ways to take attendance, I would recommend scheduling a volunteer or two (depending on the size of your worship gathering) to make note of attendance from the back of the worship space once the service starts rather than passing around an attendance folder or form to be filled out.[3] This helps to avoid any unnecessary awkwardness or discomfort a visitor might feel over having to give out their information. Keeping track of attendance on a weekly basis is incredibly helpful for shepherding purposes because it allows leaders to make note of and follow up with those who are absent or becoming increasingly inconsistent in their attendance.

Pursue visitors and guests with intentional care. Most visitors give a church plant one chance. That's it. One chance to see whether there is any real potential for them and their families to be part of this new congregation. As much as we wish it were not, this is the reality. However, this does not need to be a source of discouragement—it can be an exciting opportunity. The beautiful thing about a church plant is that it is very difficult for new people to hide or be missed. This is why pursuing visitors and guests with intentional care on Sunday mornings is so important. There is no excuse in a church plant for a visitor not to feel warmly welcomed and encouraged to become part of

3. Optional visitor cards can also be useful.

the new congregation. This is often where intentional, personal shepherding begins for new attendees of a church plant.

What might this look like in practical terms? One way to welcome visitors would be to create a culture in which they are invited to go to lunch with others after church on Sundays. Or, if lunch doesn't work, visitors could be invited to get coffee with someone in the congregation the following week. The point is to be mindful to help new people to feel truly welcomed and wanted by those in the congregation.

As for the pastor, it should be his goal to greet and welcome with joy any and every visitor who walks through the doors on Sundays. This cannot be an afterthought. This kind of loving engagement of visitors and guests must be a top priority. His enthusiasm will set the tone for the rest of the congregation by showing what it looks like to love outsiders.

Set Aside a "Shepherding Block" in the Weekly Schedule

One of the challenges many planters face is that of learning how to use their time wisely throughout the week. For this reason, it is important for a church planter to set aside a shepherding block in his weekly schedule. By this I mean a chunk of time, two to four hours each week, during which a pastor can focus solely on addressing shepherding needs in the congregation. I would recommend using this weekly shepherding block to do three things.

Call or text words of encouragement and thanks. Very few things are as powerful in the lives of Christians as loving encouragement from their pastors. As Ephesians 4:29 instructs us, "Let no corrupting talk come out of your mouths, but only such as is good for building up, as fits the occasion, that it may give grace to those who hear." Encouraging the flock, building them up with our words, should be one of the great joys of every church planter.

A shepherding block is a perfect time to think of individuals who need a quick phone call or a text message with words of encouragement. Letting people know that you love them, that God is using them, that you are thankful for their ministry, and that they are an important part of your church plant is crucial in building love and trust with your congregation.

Follow up with visitors. Setting aside a shepherding block also helps to make sure that new visitors are intentionally followed up on. Using some of this time to write a note, send an email, shoot a text message, or call a new visitor is incredibly powerful. By simply letting them know the pastor or another leader would love to buy them lunch or coffee and hear more of their story, a church plant can show personal love and care in a way that is often missed in larger congregations.

Pray for the flock. Many church planters say they have a strong desire to be in prayer for their congregations, but they struggle to make it happen because they are so busy with other responsibilities throughout the week. Setting aside a shepherding block helps a pastor to create the space he needs to regularly pray for the flock, both members and visitors alike.

Schedule at Least Three to Four Shepherding Meetings a Week

Any effective shepherding strategy begins with the pastor knowing the people who are under his pastoral care. As Tim Witmer writes, "Before a shepherd can provide proper care he must know the *identification* of the sheep for whom he is responsible. Jesus not only identifies himself as the good shepherd, but also says, 'I know My sheep and My sheep know Me' (John 10:14)."[4] It is impossible for the church planter to properly feed, lead, and protect the people God has entrusted to him if he doesn't first know who they are. Know their hurts, their pains, their hopes, and their fears. Know their stories. Know their hearts.

To know God's people, a planter must prioritize regular meetings to be with, care for, and spiritually nurture and disciple those in the congregation. For the called pastor, this should be a delight, not simply a duty. But it still takes intentionality. It takes time.

My encouragement is for a leader to schedule at least three to four shepherding meetings a week. These meetings, one to two hours in length, should focus on individuals, couples, or families who are committed members or regular attenders of the congregation. A pastor will surely have meetings with visitors and new attenders on a regular basis as well, but he must be careful not to neglect those who make up the core of the congregation.

The Joy of Shepherding a Church Plant

Church planting is hard work. It just is. And while many important responsibilities can consume a church-planting pastor's time on a weekly basis, *nothing* is more important to the growth, health, and long-term sustainability of a new congregation than intentional, biblical shepherding. Like my friend John, may we see increasing numbers of faithful planters being filled with the God-glorifying passion to know, feed, lead, and protect the flock with the heart of Christ. What a privilege and joy it is to shepherd the people of God!

4. Timothy Z. Witmer, *The Shepherd Leader: Achieving Effective Shepherding in Your Church* (Phillipsburg, NJ: P&R Publishing, 2010), 109.

USER GUIDE

SHEPHERDING IN CHURCH PLANTS

WHEN WE THINK of church planting, what often comes to mind is evangelism. And rightly so, since the purpose of church planting is to multiply churches that are filled with new followers of Jesus Christ.

But who is caring for the folks who come? If you are in a church plant or part of a church-planting network, consider how shepherding is integrated into the strategy *from the very beginning.* Ordinarily, sheep who are well cared for will not wander.

For Further Reflection

1. Do you have an intentional, comprehensive shepherding strategy? In what ways does it resemble the strategy described in this chapter? In what ways does it differ? How might you better incorporate shepherding into the mission and vision of your church?

2. How well do you know your sheep? How have you gotten to know your congregation on a micro level? How might you improve this practice?

3. Ask yourself honestly: Do you tend to enlist or shepherd volunteers? What results have you seen from your approach?

4. How can you make time for a "shepherding block" in your weekly schedule? What threatens to steal time from it? Who can you potentially empower to take on delegated tasks so that you can set aside time for shepherding?

9

SHEPHERDING AND THE GOSPEL CALL

TIMOTHY Z. WITMER

The sheep of Christ are in three states, widely different from each other. One part are not yet in the fold, and know nothing of the Good Shepherd, that bought them with his blood. Another part are in the church, or at least in a state of grace and hear the voice of the Shepherd and follow him; but are still liable to many diseases and disasters, and exposed to many fierce and powerful enemies. The third class are safely gathered into the general fold above, and feast in celestial pastures, where no ravening beast enters, and where they are exempt from all diseases, and from all danger.[1]

The primary focus of shepherding is to care for the second group of sheep Princeton professor Archibald Alexander describes

1. Archibald Alexander, "The Pastoral Office," in *Princeton and the Work of the Christian Ministry*, ed. James M. Garretson (Edinburgh: Banner of Truth Trust, 2012), 1:253.

above: those who "are in the church." Accordingly, this has been the primary focus of the chapters in this book.

But what about the first group? How do people move from "[knowing] nothing about the Good Shepherd" to being among those who "hear the voice of the Shepherd and follow him"? A question that has arisen since the publication of *The Shepherd Leader* is "Where does evangelism fit into church leaders' plans and responsibilities?" After all, it is the responsibility of the elders to admit to church membership *only* those who have heard and responded in repentance and faith to the call of the Good Shepherd.[2] How is the good news to reach the ears and hearts of those who don't know him? It can be argued that evangelism and missions should be part of the strategic leadership of the congregation as a whole.[3] But what does this look like?

In order for sheep who are not yet in the fold to "hear the voice of the Shepherd and follow him," the church must extend the loving, gracious, and compelling call of the Good Shepherd to these sheep. *We* are the ones through whom people "hear the voice of the Shepherd." As Paul wrote to the Romans, "I am not ashamed of the gospel, for it is the power of God for salvation to everyone who believes, to the Jew first and also to the Greek" (Rom. 1:16).

Our Confidence

We can take great encouragement from the fact that whenever people respond to the gospel call, they do so not because

---

2. See Timothy Z. Witmer, *The Shepherd Leader: Achieving Effective Shepherding in Your Church* (Phillipsburg, NJ: P&R Publishing, 2010), 110.

3. See Witmer, 157.

we are so articulate or because they are so smart but because their salvation is part of God's sovereign plan. "My sheep hear my voice, and I know them, and they follow me" (John 10:27).

The many who respond do so because they have been given to the Son by the Father and "hear" his voice when the gospel is shared. Describing the Gentiles' response to the preaching of Paul and Barnabas, Luke writes that "as many as were appointed to eternal life believed" (Acts 13:48). In these words the eternal plan and the human response are brought together, and this human response is linked to the faithful preaching of the gospel. Jesus has ordained the end and the means. The end is his sheep's response of faith. The means is the faithful ministry of the gospel.

Our Commission

"Scattering the seed" is one of several metaphors that Jesus uses to describe the church's act of carrying the gospel to the world. In probably the best-known example, the parable of the soils, Jesus compares various responses to the gospel to various types of soil (soil along the path, rocky soil, thorny soil, and good soil), with the good soil representing a fruitful response.

A less familiar parable that uses this metaphor appears in Mark 4:26–29. Jesus again describes a farmer scattering the seed, which we know to be God's Word. But, in this instance, although Jesus acknowledges the participation of the farmer, his focus is on the mystery of the seed's growth.

> The kingdom of God is as if a man should scatter seed on the ground. He sleeps and rises night and day, and the seed sprouts and grows; he knows not how. The earth produces by itself, first the blade, then the ear, then the full grain in the ear. But

when the grain is ripe, at once he puts in the sickle, because the harvest has come.

Although we know more about fertilization and germination than farmers did centuries ago, we still experience a sense of wonder when we see how fields planted with tiny seeds go on to produce a flourishing harvest. "The seed sprouts and grows," but the farmer "knows not how."

We have to admit that we are sometimes surprised by the people in whose lives the gospel bears fruit. "The wind blows where it wishes, and you hear its sound, but you do not know where it comes from or where it goes. So it is with everyone who is born of the Spirit" (John 3:8). The regenerating power of the Spirit cultivates the Word that is sown, bringing about life according to God's sovereign plan. J. I. Packer reminds us, "We must learn to rest all our hopes of fruit in evangelism upon the omnipotent grace of God."[4]

Jesus is clear, however, that sowing the seed and putting in the sickle are important elements in the process. In God's infinite wisdom, he has given the church that responsibility. The problem for many is that we are looking for a harvest without sowing the seed. We are looking for conversions without doing *our* part. Imagine that you look out into your garden and say to your wife, "I don't see any string beans coming up." She responds, "Dear, we didn't plant string beans this year." That is our situation when we fail to scatter the seed.

Is your church failing to see conversion growth? Go ahead, take a look at your membership rolls from the past five years and see how many have joined your church by profession of faith. If

4. J. I. Packer, *Evangelism and the Sovereignty of God* (repr., Downers Grove, IL: Intervarsity Press, 2008), 112.

you see none or very few, is the reason that you haven't developed a strategy for sowing the gospel seed?

Yes, there is an important difference between the agricultural and the spiritual. A farmer can be fairly confident that if seed is sown in properly cultivated soil and weather conditions are right, there will be a successful harvest. When we sow the seed of the Word, we do not know in whom the seed will bear fruit. But one thing is for sure: where there is no sowing, there will be no harvest. Another thing is certain: where the gospel is faithfully sown, the Lord will bring about his harvest according to his sovereign plan.

Our Cop-Outs

What are the problems that lead us to neglect this important responsibility? Consider the following "farmers" who have forgotten the essential dynamics of the harvest.

There are the *seed-saving farmers*, who think it's a lot easier to care for the seed when they keep it in their barns. They want to perfect their gospel presentations before they take them out into the world. You ask, "When are you going to scatter some of that seed?" The answer? "It's not ready!" Yes, we must make sure that the gospel we proclaim is the true gospel and is faithful to the Scriptures, but we must get out there and scatter it as well. Our presentations will never be perfect.

Then there are the *field-focused farmers*. They are out there working the soil, and they even get around to plowing some rows. You ask, "When are you going to scatter the seed?" The answer? "Not yet—the soil is not quite ready. It needs more work." These are the people who have a high profile of community involvement and service but never quite get around to scattering the seed of the gospel. Mercy ministry and community service are good, but we must be sure that we connect Word with deed. Our loving actions must eventually lead to the loving communication of the propositional truth of the gospel.

There are the *crop-swapping farmers*. These farmers are bringing crops into their barns, but these crops have been harvested by others. They may show impressive yields from year to year, but, truth be told, they are benefiting from the labors of other farmers. The reality is that these days very few churches in the United States are seeing growth through profession of faith. Much growth is simply the result of believers transferring from one church to another.[5] Now, not all transfer growth is bad. But Michael Niebauer reminds us, "We shouldn't think ourselves gifted evangelists or as having 'cracked the code' of evangelism when the bulk of our new members are a product of ecclesial migration."[6] The church that lives by the transfer can also die by the transfer.

Farsighted farmers are farmers who are looking to sow in distant fields through others. There are several difficulties for farsighted farmers, including the cost of getting the seed to those distant

5. During and immediately following the COVID pandemic, most churches rightly directed their attention inward as they focused on determining who was in and who was out. But the pandemic also amplified the problem of crop-swapping (or "sheep shuffling") as people sought out churches that followed protocols with which they were most comfortable. Any growth immediately following the pandemic was likely the result of transfer growth. Yet even before the pandemic, Lifeway Research surveyed one thousand churches and discovered that "only 6 percent to 7.5 percent [were] growing through conversions." Thom S. Rainer, "5 Realities of Evangelism in North American Churches," Lifeway Research, October 4, 2017, https://research.lifeway.com/2017/10/04/5-realities-of-churches-in-north-america/. Sheep shuffling is not a new problem.

6. Michael Niebauer, "Don't Mistake Transfer Growth for Evangelism," The Gospel Coalition, March 13, 2019, https://www.thegospelcoalition.org/article/mistake-transfer-growth-evangelism/.

places, the time it takes to understand the conditions that are most beneficial to a harvest there, and the need to hire farmers to work those fields. Nothing is wrong with wishing to see a fruitful harvest in distant places, but it can lead farmers to neglect their immediate fields. I am speaking, of course, of those who are zealous to invest in foreign missions but have not demonstrated the same commitment to scattering the seed in their local communities. Jesus told his disciples, "You will receive power when the Holy Spirit has come upon you, and you will be my witnesses in Jerusalem and in all Judea and Samaria, and to the end of the earth" (Acts 1:8). Not only does he promise that his disciples will be empowered to carry out this mission, but he also describes a *progression* to the mission. Jerusalem comes first. How are you doing in reaching your own "Jerusalem"? If we don't reach our Jerusalems, we will have no resources to invest in fields beyond our homes.

What Can You Do?

In the words of the famous military strategist Sun Tzu, "Tactics without strategy is the noise before defeat." If there is lots of independent activity but no plan, the activity may simply be a spinning of wheels that results in little productivity. Unfortunately, in many churches the situation is even worse: there is very little evangelistic activity at all.

As leaders, we are called to "equip the saints for the work of ministry" (Eph. 4:12). A plan for evangelism starts on the macro level as we work intentionally to engage and equip the entire congregation.

Emphasize the gospel. As we have seen throughout this book, proactive shepherding enables elders to know the spiritual condition of their flocks and to minister to them accordingly. There are many people who, despite sitting under faithful preaching and teaching, do not believe the gospel or else believe the gospel but continue to focus on their good deeds rather than on the finished work of Jesus Christ. On a macro level, our strategy for evangelism begins with reminding ourselves and our flocks of the complete insufficiency of our works and the complete sufficiency of our Lord's work on our behalf. It is only for this reason that we can have the assurance that Jesus speaks of in John 10.

> I give them eternal life, and they will never perish, and no one will snatch them out of my hand. My Father, who has given them to me, is greater than all, and no one is able to snatch them out of the Father's hand. I and the Father are one. (vv. 28–30)

In the last phrase we have the concurrence of the Godhead in both the accomplishment and the assurance of our salvation. The sheep are not only secure in the hand of the Good Shepherd but also nestled in the loving grasp of the Father. This is real security! But this assurance belongs only to those who have responded to the effectual call of the Good Shepherd through the gospel.

Preach Christ-centered sermons. Related to the point above, we must not forget the power of the gospel in the preaching of the Word. The apostle Paul wrote,

> How then will they call on him in whom they have not believed? And how are they to believe in him of whom they have never heard? And how are they to hear without someone preaching? And how are they to preach unless they are sent? As it is written, "How beautiful are the feet of those who preach the good news!" (Rom. 10:14–15)

Listeners should be clearly introduced to the glory of Jesus in *every* sermon. This doesn't mean a perfunctory, formulaic gospel presentation should be tacked on to every sermon. Rather, the preacher must wisely consider the legitimate, organic, textual connection of his passage to the good news.

In his Easter afternoon conversation with two disciples on the road to Emmaus, Jesus said,

> "These are my words that I spoke to you while I was still with you, that everything written about me in the Law of Moses and the Prophets and the Psalms must be fulfilled." Then he opened their minds to understand the Scriptures, and said to them, "Thus it is written, that the Christ should suffer and on the third day rise from the dead, and that repentance for the forgiveness of sins should be proclaimed in his name to all nations, beginning from Jerusalem." (Luke 24:44–47)

Yes, the whole Bible is about Jesus! No one should ever leave a worship service without learning about the greatest gift ever given.

We should expect the scattering of the seed of the gospel to bear fruit in our preaching. It is said that a downcast minister came to Rev. Charles Spurgeon in a state of discouragement because people were not professing faith in Christ as a result of his preaching. Spurgeon replied with a question: "Do you expect someone to come to Christ every time you preach?" The man said, "No, of course not." Spurgeon said, "That's the problem." What is your expectation when you preach? It can be discouraging when there is little or no apparent response. Ordinarily, the crop does not spring up the day that the seed is planted. It is the Lord who gives the harvest in his time, but you must remember to scatter the seed of the good news faithfully and *expect* there to be a harvest of transformed lives. Believe the promise of God when he says of his Word, "It shall not return to me empty, but it shall accomplish that which I purpose, and shall succeed in the thing for which I sent it" (Isa. 55:11).

Nurture the faith of children. As we care for the families in our congregations, we need to water the seed of the Word that has been planted in the hearts of our children. In Reformed congregations, children are recognized as participants in the covenant community who have the privilege of being nurtured in Christian homes and loving congregations. As part of our shepherding ministry, we should assist parents in communicating the good news to their children so that they can understand and believe.[7] When children profess their faith, it is truly a time to celebrate.

Equip your people. Once we have planted the good news in our congregations, we can begin to equip them to share the good news with others. There are many circumstances in which church members may have the opportunity to share the gospel with people they know. Perhaps a neighbor will ask a question that provides an open door. Or a coworker might ask about the source of a believer's strength and integrity. Are your members equipped to share the gospel with them? Or must they direct the inquirer to a member of the pastoral staff? One of the resources that, in my experience over the years, has been most useful for equipping members is Evangelism Explosion.[8] This ministry provides

7. A book I highly recommend for instructing children in the faith is Marian M. Schoolland, *Leading Little Ones to God: A Child's Book of Bible Teachings* (Grand Rapids: Eerdmans, 1995).

8. See www.evangelismexplosion.org. Sometimes folks push back on a programmatic approach like Evangelism Explosion's. When I hear such concerns, I ask, "What are you using instead?" More often than not, this question is met with a blank stare.

a simple, clear, and accurate outline of the gospel, and during training the learner ideally observes a live gospel presentation being made to a real person. The goal is to equip church members to share the gospel with their relatives, friends, neighbors, and coworkers as the Lord provides opportunity.

This is not where our work ends. We want to see everyone in our congregations gripped with a concern to reach the lost.

Encourage your flock to pray for the people in their circle of influence. Even if folks are not confident about sharing the good news, they can pray for others. Encourage members to develop a list of people in whose lives they would like to see the gospel take root and then to intercede for them regularly.

Provide corporate opportunities for outreach. Several years ago, All Souls Church in London, England, developed a hospitality-based ministry called Christianity Explored.[9] This ministry provides gospel-themed videos that lead to an opportunity for questions and discussion. The materials are suitable for use in a small-group home setting or a larger church-wide setting. In a congregation I served, we gathered every Wednesday night to enjoy a covered-dish dinner, watch the videos, and have small-group discussions around the tables. This was a wonderful way to involve members of the church in outreach. It also firmed up the faith of many who attended.

Be ready to welcome visitors. This begins with the Sunday morning worship service. I am not advocating a "seeker sensitive" service but a "seeker aware" service in which visitors can expect a warm welcome and not to be distracted by dirty bathrooms or

9. See www.christianityexplored.org.

the "stranger stare." The preacher should also be prepared with a Bible-based, gospel-centered, well-applied sermon. Let's not forget that the Word is the seed that bears fruit unto life (1 Peter 1:23). You should also be prepared with a follow-up strategy for visitors. Do they receive a welcome letter or email? Is there an assimilation plan to help them to move from being "inquirers" to committed followers of Jesus Christ? Every visitor is a gift from God and should be carefully cared for.

Develop an outward face for your existing ministries. Your church already has several important ministries in place. Encourage members to invite people to them. Be sure that your ministries to children, youth, men, women, and so on have an outward focus. Find ways to promote these ministries to your community—such as through social media and especially through winsome invitations from your congregants. We often forget what wonderful opportunities our existing ministries provide for reaching out to others.

The Joy When the Lost Are Found

One of the greatest joys for a church is to see the lost being found. In Luke 15, Jesus tells parables about a lost sheep, a lost coin, and a lost son. When each is found, joy results! The shepherd calls his neighbors together and says, "Rejoice with me, for I have found my sheep that was lost" (v. 6). The woman also "calls together her friends and neighbors, saying, 'Rejoice with me, for I have found the coin that I had lost'" (v. 9). And no one can forget the father's deep joy when his son returns home. He tells his servants, "'This my son was dead, and is alive again; he was lost, and is found.' And they began to celebrate (v. 24).

Moreover, after recounting the shepherd's joy, Jesus says, "Just so, I tell you, there will be more joy in heaven over one sinner who repents than over ninety-nine righteous persons who need no repentance" (v. 7). In the wake of the earthly celebration over the lost coin that is found, Jesus says, "Just so, I tell you, there is joy before the angels of God over one sinner who repents" (v. 10).

Fewer things bring greater joy to the community of faith than seeing someone profess their faith in Jesus Christ. When this happens, prayers are answered, and lives are changed before our very eyes. This kind of joy should motivate elders to equip and mobilize their flocks to extend the gospel call to those in their sphere of influence.

USER GUIDE

Your Evangelism Track Record

SET ASIDE SOME time to review the list of the new members your church has welcomed over the past five years. In all honesty, how many of your new members are joining by transfer rather than by profession of faith?

Next, ask yourself whether the elders of your church are personally confident in their ability to share the gospel with someone in (or outside) their flock and to lead them to Christ.

Consider investing in materials or training that would build up your congregation's confidence in witnessing to the gospel. Are you aware of what other churches in your area are using?

For Further Reflection

1. When was the last time that *you* personally shared the good news with another person?
2. Is evangelism part of the strategy of your church? Why or why not?

3. What practical steps can you take to equip your people to share their faith?
4. How might you involve everyone in your congregation in the outreach of the church?

RECOMMENDED RESOURCES

Byrd, Aimee. *No Little Women: Equipping All Women in the Household of God.* Phillipsburg, NJ: P&R Publishing, 2016.

Croft, Brian. *The Pastor's Ministry: Biblical Priorities for Faithful Shepherds.* Grand Rapids: Zondervan, 2015.

Doriani, Dan. *Women and Ministry: What the Bible Teaches.* Wheaton, IL: Crossway, 2003.

Eclov, Lee. *Pastoral Graces: Reflections on the Care of Souls.* Chicago: Moody Publishers, 2012.

Ferguson, Sinclair B. *Devoted to God: Blueprints for Sanctification.* Carlisle, PA: Banner of Truth, 2016.

Martin, Albert N. *Pastoral Theology,* vol. 3, *The Man of God: His Shepherding, Evangelizing, and Counseling Labors.* Montville, NJ: Trinity Pulpit Press, 2020.

Mitchell, Matthew C. *Resisting Gossip: Winning the War of the Wagging Tongue.* Fort Washington, PA: CLC Publications, 2013.

Schlichting, Randy, with Bob Carter and Herschel Hatcher. *Like Sheep with a Shepherd: A Primer for Elders in the Church.* 6th ed. Scotts Valley, CA: CreateSpace, 2017.

Senkbeil, Harold L. *The Care of Souls: Cultivating a Pastor's Heart.* Bellingham, WA: Lexham Press, 2019.

Strauch, Alexander. *Leading with Love.* Littleton, CO: Lewis and Roth Publishers, 2006.

Thomas, Scott, and Tom Wood. *Gospel Coach: Shepherding Leaders to Glorify God*. Grand Rapids: Zondervan, 2012.

Tripp, Paul David. *Instruments in the Redeemer's Hands: People in Need of Change Helping People in Need of Change*. Phillipsburg, NJ: P&R Publishing, 2002.

Witmer, Timothy Z. *The Shepherd Leader: Achieving Effective Shepherding in Your Church*. Phillipsburg, NJ: P&R Publishing, 2010.

Shepherd Leader Ministries has created a digital "Shepherding Snapshot" that consists of a few short questions based on the "Seven Elements of an Effective Shepherding Ministry." This assessment allows elders to consider their perceived effectiveness in shepherding. Please write to theshepherdleader@gmail.com to receive a copy of this tool or access it at www.theshepherdleader.com.

LIST OF CONTRIBUTORS

John Barrett is the executive pastor at First Presbyterian Church (PCA) in Augusta, Georgia.

Mark Hallock (MDiv, Denver Seminary; DMin, Westminster Theological Seminary) serves as the lead pastor of Calvary Church (Southern Baptist Convention) in Englewood, Colorado. He also serves as president of the Calvary Family of Churches, an organization that is committed to planting and replanting churches for the glory of God (www.thecalvary.org). He and his wife, Jenna, have two children.

Sue Harris (MA, Reformed Theological Seminary) serves as the women's ministry director at Oak Mountain Presbyterian Church in Birmingham, Alabama. She served in Mission to the World for nine years and previously spent twelve years as a college women's basketball coach.

Ken Jones (DMin, Birmingham Theological Seminary) is senior pastor of Amelia Plantation Chapel on Amelia Island, Florida. He was shepherding pastor at Oak Mountain Presbyterian Church in Birmingham, Alabama, from 2012 to 2022 and served for over thirteen years as a deputy sheriff for the Fairfax County Sheriff's Office in Northern Virginia.

Bijan Mirtolooi (MDiv, Westminster Theological Seminary; ThM, Princeton Theological Seminary; DMin, Fuller Theological Seminary) began serving as lead pastor for Reality Church London, a vibrant church in East London, UK, in 2021. Prior to his ministry in London, Bijan served as a pastor at Redeemer Presbyterian Church West Side in New York City, where he oversaw pastoral care and community groups. Bijan and his wife, Michelle, live in East London with their two children, Esmé and Oliver.

Randy Schlichting (MDiv, Metro Atlanta Seminary; DMin, Birmingham Theological Seminary) is the pastor of shepherding at Perimeter Church (PCA), a 4,500-member church in Atlanta, Georgia. Randy also provides biblical marriage counseling as well as leadership training for officers. He has been on staff at Perimeter for twenty-five years. Randy has been married to Dorothy for over forty years. They have three grown and married daughters and six grandchildren, as well as a dog named Lucy.

Gary L. Smith is a ruling elder at Central Presbyterian Church (Evangelical Presbyterian Church) in St. Louis, Missouri, where he is also chair of the flock oversite team of the shepherding ministry and the career care ministry. He is an experienced C-level executive who has over fifty years of sales, operational, and executive leadership experience. Gary is married to Jan and has a son, Jeff, and a daughter, Julie. Jan and Gary have five grandchildren.

Timothy Z. Witmer is emeritus professor of practical theology at Westminster Theological Seminary and director of Shepherd Leader Ministries. He served in pastoral ministry in the Presbyterian Church in America for more than forty years and is the author of *The Shepherd Leader*, *The Shepherd Leader at Home*, and *Mindscape*. He has been married to Barbara since 1975, and they have three grown children and seven grandchildren.

Also from P&R Publishing

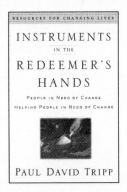

We might be relieved if God placed our sanctification only in the hands of trained professionals, but that is not his plan. Instead, through the ministry of every part of the body, the whole church will mature in Christ.

Paul David Tripp helps us discover where change is needed in our own lives and the lives of others. Following the example of Jesus, Tripp reveals how to get to know people and how to lovingly speak truth to them.

"A wonderful application of the old Gaelic saying, 'God strikes straight blows with crooked sticks.' As inadequate as we are, God is eager to use us to help others change. The more you apply the biblical principles discussed in this book, the more readily you will fit into his mighty hand."

—**Ken Sande**, author of *The Peacemaker: A Biblical Guide to Resolving Personal Conflict*

Also from P&R Publishing

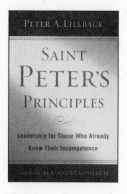

In this comprehensive handbook, Peter Lillback, president of Westminster Theological Seminary, uses the apostle Peter's life and writings to guide men and women through the details and daily challenges of leadership in any arena. Readers will think through their relationships, productivity, management style, communication, decision-making, conflict resolution, integrity, and more. Practical spiritual exercises help to put the lessons of each short section into action.

"This is a rich, wonderfully instructive and helpful compendium of wisdom on all aspects of leadership. There is nothing merely theoretical."
—**Alistair Begg**, Senior Pastor, Parkside Church, Bainbridge, Ohio

"I have never read a book on leadership quite like this one. . . . Peter Lillback's book is a treasure-house of wisdom to be digested slowly."
—**D. A. Carson**, Emeritus Professor of New Testament, Trinity Evangelical Divinity School

Also from P&R Publishing

Do you crave people's love and approval? Do you dread their condemnation, rejection, or mistreatment? Although we don't always realize it, many of our lives—and identities—are dangerously contorted around such longings and fears.

When People Are Big and God Is Small walks us through seven steps to overcoming our fear of others. Along the way, discover a fear of the Lord that, in Christ, is filled with gratitude, love, and devotion—freeing you to need others less and love them more.

This new edition of biblical counselor Edward Welch's groundbreaking work has been substantially updated and revised.

"Few books have impacted me, my family, and my church more deeply than *When People Are Big and God Is Small*. It introduces concepts—biblical truths—that have transformed the way we understand our relationships with God and man alike."
—**Tim Challies**, Blogger, www.challies.com

Was this book helpful to you?
Consider writing a review online.
The contributors appreciate your feedback!

Or write to P&R at editorial@prpbooks.com
with your comments. We'd love to hear from you.